THE BEST NANNY HANDBOOK

The Ultimate Guide for Nannies

Emma Kensington

The Best Nanny Handbook
The Ultimate Guide for Nannies

TABLE OF CONTENTS

INTRODUCTION

The Best Nanny Handbook is prepared as a general guide for nannies. My purpose of creating this book is to shed some light into common issues nannies face as well as providing the necessary day-to-day information.

This book can also be used by people who are thinking about becoming a nanny. Childcare, duties, living with strangers and millions of other questions that you can't find answers to about this career can be found here.

Being a nanny is a rewarding career and certainly requires solid knowledge of childcare and child development. It is crucial for the modern day nannies to be armed with the information provided here to raise healthy and happy children.

CHAPTER 1- WHAT IS A NANNY?

Working with children can be the most fulfilling experience of someone's life. Although many people don't realize the emotional satisfaction of being a nanny, most good nannies are well-aware of it. Raising children is a long term investment. You may not see the results of your work right away, but it is life altering. A great nanny shapes the lives of her charges, nurtures them and loves them unconditionally. It is the exceptional nanny who understands her role in the lives of others and the importance of her job.

Some nannies go through crises with the families they work for and stick with them throughout. It is not uncommon to hear about nannies who have been working with the same family for ten years, even longer. Naturally, not all days can be easy and trouble-free, but there must be a key to such successful relationship.
Nanny's responsibility hardly stops at the children. Children come with parents. After all, someone has to pay the nanny's salary. Nanny-parent relation is a close one, especially compared to other employee-employer relations. This doesn't mean they must be close friends or know every single thing about each other. This is a special employee-employer relationship where people have to work very close to make it work. There can be plenty of room for misinterpretation or misunderstanding. Only way to avoid these negativities is to keep an open and honest communication line. If the parties can not feel that they can communicate issues and problems to each other in an open and

respectful manner, the relationship is on its way to more problems. Most nannies admit that the main reason for quitting their job is the parents, not the children or the job itself. There could be some instances where parents could indeed be problematic and very demanding. But in most cases the problems stem from the lack of communication.

What is a nanny?

Nanny is a person whose primary responsibility is to take care of a family's children in their house. She is a professional child care worker and considered to be an employee of the family. We will use "she" rather than "he" throughout this book since the majority of nannies are female. A full time nanny usually works approximately 40-50 hours a week although hours can be longer depending on the employing family. Part time nannies are also in high demand as telecommuting and flexible work schedules for parents are getting more common.

Today's working parents often turn to nannies for full time, in-house child care. It is one of the best child care options for busy families as the children do not need to be dragged to the day care center at the early hours of the morning. Nanny cares for the children at the comfort of the children's home and some even lives with the family. Live-in nanny arrangement is very common among parents who work long or irregular work schedules. Generally, a live-in nanny receives free room and board; therefore, her wages might be little less than what a live-out nanny receives.

Qualities of a nanny

Contrary to popular belief, being a nanny requires a lot of hard work. Some people have the notion of this job being easy and not demanding. Needless to say, these people have no idea what it takes to care for children. Not everyone can be a nanny. It is physically and emotionally demanding. There is no room for error, especially with young children. One must be alert at all times around a baby who is just learning to walk or a curious toddler who wants to help out in the kitchen.

A nanny's responsibility is not only to provide physical care, but also to set a good role model for the developing child. Children see the adults in their lives as the most important figures. Nanny is sure one of the people the child looks up to. They learn and copy everything from table manners to speech of their caregivers.

Each and every family may have a list of the important qualities they are looking for in a nanny when they are recruiting. The list might be long or short depending on how much thought they put in to it and how experienced they are with the process. New parents may be clueless and overlook the important traits. A good nanny knows what it takes to be a nanny and what sets her apart from the rest.

Needless to say, every good nanny should have personal traits such as intelligence, good morals, common sense, and cheerful disposition. Most importantly, she should first be committed to the welfare of the children.

Below are the most important qualities a nanny or nanny candidate should have:

- **Loving and nurturing-** A good nanny must have unconditional love for children and always watch out for their well-being. Every child needs loving and nurturing adults in his life to build his self-esteem. Caregiver plays an important role in a child's life and emotional development that can last a lifetime. Children who are surrounded with nurture and kindness grow up to be happy, confident adults. They learn to treat people with respect and affection early on in their lives.

- **Good morals and manners-** Children learn by example and copy the behavior patterns of the adults around them. This applies to any type of behavior, good and bad. They look up to their nannies and assume they can do no wrong. Setting a good example and being a role model are integral parts of every nanny job. This may not be spelled out in a work agreement, but it must always be understood. Nanny should have good moral traits and manners to set an example for her charges. Only a nanny with high morals and proper manners can help her charges grow up with the same characteristics. Adults may not realize when they make an untrue statement or when they don't mean to lie, but children are hungry for information and they don't easily forget. When speaking to a child, it is important to keep in mind that he is a little person and speak to him with care and respect. This will also help child act in such manner in return. Children are greatly affected by unkind behavior and may think they are not loved if treated so.

- **Patient-** Taking care of children requires a lot of patience. A person with short temper is not suitable to be a nanny. A good nanny is the one who can patiently answer the endless questions of a preschooler or the one who can keep her composure when a toddler throws a temper tantrum.

- **Able to work long hours-** Nannies are usually required to work more than eight hours a day considering that full time working parents would need nanny to be there while they are commuting to their jobs. Most nannies don't get a real break while on duty unless children go to school or nap. Even then there might be household chores to do. Being a nanny can be an isolating job from the outside world, especially with infant charges. Most nannies are needed to work long days and must stay alert for the safety and well-being of the children.

- **Clean-** Cleanliness is a major issue especially with infants. Formula bottles, diapers, bedding, toys, clothing and high chairs must be kept clean at all times. Germs thrive on these items that children are in close contact with. Proper hygiene techniques must be applied to keep the children's environment clean and germ-free to prevent illness.

- **Organized-** School-age children typically have a number of after school activities. Sometimes just keeping these in mind can be overwhelming. Great organizational skills come in handy when the children have hectic schedules. Birthday parties, playgroups, piano practice, ballet and sports are just a few to name. In some cases, you may not only take the children to the activities, but also to coordinate them.

- **Reliable-** Working parents rely on their nannies to show up on time so that they can get to work. A good nanny understands the importance of this and takes her job seriously. She realizes parents rely on her with the schedules and the good care of their children. Showing up on time in the mornings and calling in sick in a timely manner are every responsible adult's qualities. Parents depend on you in order to do their job and support their families.

- **Trustworthy-** Parents would want to leave their children only with people they can trust. Children are their most important possession and the person who is a role model to them must be trustworthy. This is also important for a smooth parent-nanny relation. If one of the parties even has suspicions about the honesty of the other, problems will arise. In order to prevent future problems, a good nanny does not hide even the things that may seem unimportant to her. Parents appreciate the honesty and communication. They won't be overwhelmed with the abundance of the information you pass along, especially if it is on a daily log.

- **Flexible-** Most parents have a certain way of raising their children and expect nanny to follow it. Nanny and parents should be consistent with the determined discipline style. If one uses timeout and the other doesn't even approve it, it causes more confusion for the children. If the nanny can not live with the family's style, they are a mismatch. Child rearing philosophies must be discussed at the interview and the nanny should decide if she can apply the parent's wishes. It is normal to have different views; however, if a nanny strongly disagrees with the family's views, it is better that she doesn't take the job. It is impossible for a parent-nanny team to agree on everything when it comes to childcare, but a little flexibility and adaptability can only help things run more smoothly.

- **Initiative-** Most parents do not want to be bothered with telling their nanny what to do every minute of the day. Busy parents want a nanny to be a self starter. Creative and initiative nanny makes sure children make the most of their time. Educational and fun activities for any age group can be created with some effort. Even the youngest children can benefit from quality time. Keeping the children occupied and entertained while getting the must-do things done in an organized manner is a trait of a great nanny. A committed nanny is the one who creates activities to fill the day and takes the initiative to contribute to the children's development.

- **Communicative-** Open communication is the key to a successful nanny-parent team. Problems, small or big, arise even in the best of relations. The important thing is to communicate them in a professional and respectful manner. Unless the parents are made aware of the issues, they can not do anything about them. Speak up and be open about the issues concerning you even if the parents are the cause of the problems. Weekly meetings are excellent opportunities to air any problems and seek solutions. Sometimes solutions may not be so simple, but at least plans can be made to resolve them. Keeping the problems to herself will only cause a nanny to become unhappy and finally quit.

Qualifications of a nanny

There are no mandatory nanny certifications or diplomas required to qualify for a nanny job. That doesn't mean that anyone can be a nanny or easily get a job. Requirements depend on and change by each hiring family. Some families are too picky and only hire nannies with experience in the age group of their children. Some will request CPR and First Aid training before starting the job. Personal traits may be more important than CPR and First Aid certifications for some families as any nanny can be trained on these later on. Besides personal traits, some qualifications that families may require or desire are:

- **Experience-** Most families prefer experienced candidates to look after their children. In fact, nannies are usually experienced childcare workers. Beginner nannies may have some babysitter, mother's helper, au pair or similar experience in childcare. Experienced nannies have several years of paid childcare experience or experience raising their own children. To break in to the profession, it is best to work as a babysitter or mother's helper first. Then, decide if you really enjoy working with children before taking up a nanny job.

- **Driver's license-** As most families live in the suburbs nowadays, getting anywhere without a car is nearly impossible. A driver's license with a clean driving record is a great asset as most nannies will need to get to work or drive their charges around. Families with school-age children may demand driving more than families with infants.

- **CPR training-** Although not a requirement by most families, it is highly recommended that a nanny candidate gets CPR training especially if she will care for infants. Simple CPR training can save lives in case of an emergency. Also a nanny with the CPR certification may stand out in a job interview and increase her chances of getting the job. CPR training courses are offered almost anywhere in the country by the Red Cross.

- **First Aid training-** Emergencies, little cuts and bruises are a part of life. Nannies may have to deal with these issues during work hours and must be well prepared. It is imperative that a nanny knows how to treat small cuts and bruises to prevent infection. Again a nanny candidate with first aid training usually has an edge compared to a candidate without training.

- **Education-** Nannies have a wide variety of educational backgrounds. Most families would prefer a college educated nanny, preferably with a degree in early childhood development or related area. A college educated nanny can command a higher salary than a non-college graduate nanny. If the nanny is required to home school the children, a college degree is a must as she would also be responsible for the education of the children. Many great nannies may not have a four-year-college degree, but educate themselves very well through reading childcare books, magazines and industry publications.

Duties and responsibilities

Keep in mind that this is a unique job and the responsibilities may become blurred easily. You work in someone's home and perhaps live with them. Friendship between the employee and the employer is inevitable and is a good thing. When this happens, it is not uncommon for either party to slack off a little. Keeping it professional can become harder and this may bring problems. Hopefully, every nanny-parent team gathers once a week for a meeting to resolve issues and compliment each other on a job well-done.

Needless to say, well-being and safety of the children is a nanny's primary responsibility. Children require constant attention and must be supervised at all times. This applies to an infant during nap time or a preschooler watching television. Children are famous for getting in to trouble when they are not supervised.

Nanny is involved with every aspect of the children's lives. Duties can be a long list, especially with children of different age groups. Responsibilities include reading to the children, helping/supervising homework, managing the children's meals, dressing, bathing, playing, doing crafts, driving them to school and activities in some cases. With infants, the list includes diaper changing, feeding and dressing the child. Infant care involves more hands on duties as someone needs to do everything for them.

Child-related light housekeeping duties are generally a nanny's responsibilities as well. These include cleaning up the kitchen after meals and keeping the children's area tidy. Keeping the kitchen clean after meals, as well as during meal preparation, is especially very important to prevent germs and food poisoning. It is essential that the children's environment and clothes are clean. Some families may request additional tasks such as doing children's laundry, vacuuming children's areas and loading/unloading the dishwasher.

It is important to be realistic about the housework duties. Cleaning the house is not a nanny's responsibility, but a housekeeper's. Nanny's time is best spent with the children, doing educational and fun activities. Nanny should keep the children busy and help their development rather than cleaning the house. Some nannies care for only one infant or toddler who takes long naps in the morning or afternoon. In this case, some light housework can be done. A mom who comes home after a long day of work does not want to see the house in a chaos. Putting the toys away at the end of the day and putting the dishes in the dishwasher should be done no matter what. It is common courtesy.

Although some parents expect some housekeeping duties, it is imperative to discuss all the duties during the interview process. It is highly recommended to have a work agreement that spells out the duties in detail. If additional duties are added afterwards, it must be discussed and must be compensated accordingly. Most nannies complain about additional work being added to their schedules with no extra pay. They feel that they are being taken advantage of. If you find yourself in such situation, bring it up on a meeting. If you are overwhelmed with extra duties, tell the parents you don't have enough time to do the additional tasks or you can do them with additional compensation. Some parents may offer to make up for the additional work with time off. If it works for you, that's great. If not, explain them clearly the reason without being defensive or argumentative. Don't bottle it up as the consequences will lead to resentment. Resentment will lead to quitting.

Below is a list of common nanny duties:
- Get children ready in the morning
- Prepare children's meals and clean up afterwards
- Drive children to school and activities
- Assist and supervise homework
- Give children's baths
- Do children's laundry
- Change and launder children's sheets
- Iron children's clothes
- Keep children's bedrooms and play areas tidy
- Vacuum children's bedrooms and play areas
- Participate in playgroup activities
- Run errands related to children
- Keep a grocery list
- Sweep/mop the kitchen floor
- Load and empty dishwasher
- Empty trash

Salary
Even though most families and nannies have a figure in mind in terms of the salary, they should discuss and determine the salary together. Many factors should be considered when negotiating the nanny salary. They should be carefully weighted out to come up with a number. Full time nanny salaries can vary between $250 and $800 or more per week depending on all the factors discussed below. It is recommended that you do a market research in your area to find out what the going rate is. You can call the local nanny agencies or talk to the other nannies in the area. Most experienced nannies know the going rate and demand certain salary. Nannies just like anyone else have bills to pay. If you are not flexible about the salary, make sure the family knows it early on.

This will save you time to eliminate the families who can not simply afford you.

You should also discuss how you will handle the taxes. Nanny is an employee of the family and appropriate payroll taxes, Medicare and social security taxes, should be paid by the nanny and the family. Family pays half of the Medicare and social security taxes and can cut the other half from the nanny's paycheck upon nanny's request. Nanny is responsible for her federal income tax, but the family can withhold this tax from the paycheck and deposit it along with payroll taxes. Actually, it is best if you ask them to withhold your federal income tax from your paycheck if you don't want to end up with a hefty tax bill on April 15. State and/or federal unemployment tax must be paid by the family and/or nanny depending on the state. Beware that all appropriate taxes must be paid by the family and the nanny just like any other job for legal employment. An accountant can easily set up the paychecks including all the necessary taxes. A number of families assume that nannies are always paid under the table. Naturally, this arrangement is more economical for both parties. Nanny keeps all her wages, family does not pay anything extra to the government. It sounds like a fair arrangement. However, a professional nanny should think about the future. Retirement, unemployment, disability insurance are all things most people don't want to think about not to forget getting caught by the IRS.

Following factors contribute to the nanny salary:

- **Number of hours worked-** Are going to work full time or part time? Naturally, a part time nanny should be paid less than a full time nanny. Generally, an hourly wage for the nanny is determined considering all other factors. Hourly wage is then multiplied by the number of hours worked in a week. A minimum number of hours must be set for every week. If one week the family doesn't require your services for a few hours or even a day through no fault of your own, you should be paid for that time as well. You should be paid for the agreed amount of hours each day if you are ready and available to work.

- **Location-** Nanny salaries vary greatly by the region in the United States. This is one of the most important factors as the nanny salaries are much higher in the big metropolitan areas than rural areas. This is a very important factor, especially in live out situations, as the housing expenses fluctuate greatly throughout the country. A good rule of thumb is to find out what the going rate range is in the neighborhood or the town where the family lives. You will be surprised to find out how big of a gap there is between rural and metropolitan areas.

- **Responsibilities-** Are you going to take care of the children only or are you going to help with the housekeeping as well? How many children are there? What are the exact duties expected of the nanny? The more children you care for, the higher the salary should be.

  Although most nannies are responsible for childcare and children-related light housekeeping, some nannies may be responsible for more. If other tasks, such as; general housekeeping, running errands and grocery shopping are a part of the nanny's responsibilities, compensation must be higher accordingly.

- **Live-in or live-out-** If you live with the family, you should expect to be paid less than a live out nanny. Live-in arrangement usually includes free private room and board. Nanny would not have to pay for housing and food which may be quite significant in some metropolitan areas. Even then the family should not decrease the pay of the nanny significantly; it is usually very convenient to have a live-in nanny for the families who choose to do so. In addition, it doesn't cost the family extra to have someone living in a spare bedroom. Food and utility expenses are usually insignificant unless you have a special diet, organic etc. Some families may even offer to pay the same amount to both live-in and live-out nannies.

- **Experience-** Nannies are usually experienced childcare workers unlike babysitters. A nanny who has five years of experience would command a higher salary than a nanny with a year of experience. If there are very young children to be taken care of, experience with this age group is a critical factor.

- **Education-** Most professional nannies have a high school degree or higher. Some even have a college degree in a related field or a master's degree. Naturally, the more education a nanny has the higher salary she would command. If tutoring for school-age children is required, you should be compensated more than if you didn't tutor the children.

- **Overtime-** Federal Fair Labor Standards Act states that workers who work in excess of 40 hours a week must be compensated for the extra hours at time and a half. This applies to live-out nannies only. Live-in nannies must also be paid for the extra hours, but not necessarily at time and a half.

Benefits

It is not unlawful or uncommon for families not to offer nannies any benefits. However, they are an important part of the total compensation package and a great way to keep a great nanny. Benefits give workers sense of security. Make sure you discuss and understand them before accepting a job. Benefits do actually have monetary value which most people don't see, especially the health benefits. Think of the entire salary and benefit package together as a whole when considering a job offer.

Following are the common benefits most professional nannies receive:

- **Paid vacation-** You should expect to be compensated 52 weeks a year including minimum of two weeks of paid vacation. You should be paid for the time not worked if the time missed is not a fault of your own. For example, if the family decides to take a three day weekend and you get the Friday off, you should be paid your whole paycheck for that week.

- **Holidays-** New Years Day, Presidents Day, Memorial Day, 4th of July, Labor Day, Thanksgiving Day and Christmas Day are the traditional holidays and most people get them off with pay in the corporate world. Chances are your employers will as well. Your services probably won't be needed on these days; however, you should be receiving your income.

- **Sick days-** Nanny is entitled to sick days even though it is not illegal if she doesn't get any sick days. Usually, around five paid days of sick leave a year is considered fair.

- **Health insurance-** It is recommended for the families to provide and pay for the health insurance of their nanny in full. Some families may want to start out with sharing the cost of the health insurance in half with the nanny. They gradually take over the entire cost if things go well. Even if the family offers to contribute a smaller portion of it, get health insurance. No matter what, this is an important benefit to have considering the skyrocketing healthcare costs.

- **Raise-** Just like any other professional, nanny expects a yearly performance review and a raise based on the performance review. Pay increases are a nice way of showing appreciation. A performance review followed by a 3%-5% pay raise is a typical yearly increase for the nanny profession. If you live in a very expensive area or want higher raises, you must discuss and include it in your work agreement.

Live-in vs. live-out

A live-in nanny is a nanny who lives with the family in their house. She is provided with a free private bedroom and board in addition to her salary. Typically, live-in nanny arrangement best suits parents who work irregular hours, travel for business or commute long hours. Nowadays, a number of other families who work regular 9 to 5 jobs like to hire live-in nannies as well. With a live-in nanny, parents would never have to worry about nanny arriving on time or arriving at all in the morning. She lives in the next room and takes her only a minute to get to work! Sick days or bad weather would not be a big concern as the nanny would not have to drive to work.

Live-in nannies are provided with their own private bedroom and a private bathroom in most cases. It would be foolish to think that nanny could share a bedroom with one of the children. It is just not acceptable and would cause problems down the line. After a long day with the children, every nanny is entitled to her own down time and should not be disturbed by the members of the family during her off hours. Appropriate rest and quiet time are necessary to prevent burnout and recharge for the next busy work day.

Any nanny can be a live-in nanny, but this arrangement is more popular among nannies who relocate from another town. It makes perfect sense to move in with the family rather than looking for a place to live and furniture. Living with the family can save time, money and effort. It can also help her build a social life as the family can help her get acquainted with their social circle.

Live-in nannies save money on rent, utilities, transportation costs, and food. Even though a live-in nanny may earn a bit less than a live-out nanny, financial benefits are still there. In some areas, housing costs can be extremely high and can take up a big chunk of a nanny's salary. Free housing can save a nanny considerable amount of money especially in the expensive areas; such as, San Francisco, Los Angeles, Washington, D.C. or New York. Most families pay live-in and live-out nannies almost the same amount. However, generally live-in nannies get paid a little less. It is unacceptable for a family to calculate how much the nanny would pay for room and board if she had lived out and deduct the amount from her wages. Families should keep in mind that having a live-in nanny has its great benefits for them and should pay a fair wage just like they would to a live-out nanny. Under normal circumstances, it doesn't cost the family too much extra to provide a room and board for the live-in nanny.

One should keep in mind that a live-in nanny doesn't leave the house after work. She lives with the family in their house. This arrangement may not suit a nanny who wants total privacy after work or a person who like to have visitors over often. There are privacy issues to be considered with a live-in arrangement. Having another adult living in the house can be uncomfortable for some people. Unless the family has separate living quarters for the nanny, privacy can be an issue for everyone.

Live-in arrangement gives a chance to families and nannies to get to know each other better. This can be a great opportunity for a healthy family-nanny relationship.

It would be unrealistic not to think through the advantages and disadvantages of both arrangements. Every nanny candidate should consider her own circumstances to decide if live-in or live-out situation is ideal for her before even starting to look for a job. Each party should review the benefits and the disadvantages of live-in versus live-out arrangement and decide on the best option for them.

CHAPTER 2 - FINDING A NANNY JOB

Resume

Most nannies don't think it is important to have a resume. There is nothing wrong with having a resume and updating it from time to time. Each job is different and comes with a new set of responsibilities. It is essential have a record of what you have done in your previous jobs.

Keep track of your professional achievements with your resume. Update it when you undertake a new job and new responsibilities. Take it with you when you go to a job interview. Parents will be impressed by how serious you are about your job. Leave a copy for them to look through after the interview. This will give you a competitive edge compared to the other candidates without a resume.

Where to look for jobs

Most people have the impression that the best jobs come from the nanny agencies. Unfortunately, this is not true. Good jobs can be found in a number of places, they are not only hidden in the nanny agency files. Agencies are usually preferred by busy families who don't have the time to do background or reference checks on their own. Families pay an application fee and a large placement fee to those agencies. Typical placement fees run as high as first month's salary. Some families may feel unhappy about that and in turn offer a smaller salary to the nanny. There are also benefits of an agency. First of all, they serve the nannies for free. It doesn't cost anything to register with one to keep your options open. They also find you another job for you if things don't work out. Keep in mind that agencies are eager to place nannies fast and some of them will not be thorough about the matching process. Only you can determine whether a job is a good fit for you or not.

Experienced nannies usually befriend other nannies in the playgroups or in the neighborhoods they work in. It is always a good idea to develop a network of friends with a common interest. It helps not only professional development, but also recommendations for new jobs when you need one. Almost always a nanny knows a family in need of child care. And the parents prefer recommendations from people they know. Keeping your circle of nanny friends can help you when you need it the most.

Newspaper advertisements are considered the traditional way of looking for any job. The prospects and results can be great through these ads. The important part is to read the advertisement well. Do you fit all the criteria? Only answer the ads where you fit the job description. Ads are usually quite short and most families may not answer the phone calls for the reasons of prescreening over the answering machine. This may not sound fair, but do leave a message on the machine with clear instructions. Speak slowly and leave your full name, phone number and the hours you can be reached.

Phenomenal growth of the Internet now allows people to find jobs online. These could be through classified ad sites or special nanny job sites. They usually work like classified ads, but more information can be available saving you time on the telephone interview.

Telephone interview

Nowadays people are busier than ever and do not have the time to have a face-to-face interview with every prospect. This also applies to the nannies. Chances are you will be working a full time job when you are looking for a new one. This is when the phone interview comes in handy. It is a great way to prescreen jobs before investing your time to go to someone's house.

Setup a time slot for this interview when you won't have to rush to finish up the interview. Remember this is your first interview and first impression. You can only make a first impression once and it might be particularly difficult to make a good one over the phone; so be prepared. Review the nanny interview questions and go through your answers to prepare for the interview. Take notes on a piece of paper about your strengths and special talents. These could be hard to remember during the phone interview.

Don't hesitate to ask questions. Ask about anything that is important to you. This shows the family that you take your job seriously and you are really interested in a good family-nanny match. You should ask questions about the childcare duties, housekeeping duties, exact schedule, salary, benefits and childcare philosophy. Listen to the answers carefully and take quick notes. Learn the children's names and use them during the phone interview. After the basics are answered, you will have an idea if the job may fit you. If you are interested, express your interest in the job. If the family sees a potential match, they may schedule a face-to-face interview before they hang up. Some experienced families may go through all the phone interviews first with all the nanny candidates and in the next round schedule the in person interviews.

Speak clearly, not too fast, not too slow. Be pleasant and polite. Choose your words carefully, use proper English and avoid any type of slang. Be prepared to ask your questions as well. It is highly recommended to have them written down and to take notes.

Job application

If you are interviewing a family who has had nannies in the past, it is very possible that they will ask you to fill out a job application. Do not be alarmed. Every professional work place asks for a candidate to fill out an application. If the family does the same, this shows how serious they take the job and their nanny. This is generally a good sign; however, don't pass the job if they don't. Most families are new to the hiring process or they don't do it very often. That's one of the reasons to have a resume handy. You can have something to leave behind and what better than a well-written resume.

Interview

Being prepared for the interview is the best thing you can do to make a great impression. Family will appreciate the fact that you are an organized nanny candidate and you take your job seriously. You are off to a good start if you show up with a list of questions, references, resume, and the copies of your certifications if you have any.

Review the most common questions parents ask at the nanny interviews. Memorize everyone's name in the household and go through the telephone interview notes you had taken. If you remember everything you have learned so far about the family, you won't ask repeat questions that can be annoying. This will help you show the family you are serious about the job.

Review your strengths and think of a reason why you could make a good match for this family. Answering these questions will help you evaluate the job better. Remember a good nanny is interested in finding a job that fits her best and vice versa. You may be asked questions about your weaknesses. Think of them beforehand. Show the family that you are willing to work on your weak areas and improve them. Everyone has strong and weak points; the important thing is the willingness to learn and improve professionally.

Clean and conservative are the keywords for proper nanny job interview attire. Make sure you look professional; however, you certainly don't need a business suit. A dress or khakis with a shirt will do the job. Don't forget to iron! Do not wear anything that reveals too much, too short, tight or uncomfortable even if it is your style. Think comfortable, there is a chance that you will meet the children and you should be able to get on the floor to play with them. Avoid big jewelry and strong perfumes. Be on time!

Can I take a friend with me to the interview?
If you don't feel comfortable going to a stranger's house alone, you should kindly tell the family that you would feel better if you could bring a friend along. There is nothing wrong with this and the family should understand your concern. You can alternatively hold the first interview in a public place like a coffee house, then setup another meeting in their house. Tell at least one friend that you are going for a nanny job interview and leave the family's address with them.

After the interview
Sending a thank you note after the interview is not necessary, but it's a nice gesture. Families usually tell the candidates when they will make a decision and call her back. Wait until the day they are supposed to call

you. If they don't call by that day, it's okay to call them the day after to ask if they are still interested in you.

Communicate with several families at the same time. Arrange interviews and meetings with all the families you are interested in. Do not stop your nanny job search and wait around for a family to call you. If you accept a job offer, call the other families to let them know you are no longer available.

Things to discuss

This is the time to discuss everything you are wondering about the particular nanny job. It is the opportunity to determine if the job is right for you. If you think the job is perfect for you, show the family you are the best candidate for the job. Be polite and speak clearly. Answer the questions in detail; don't just give yes or no answers. If there is a question you do not understand, ask for explanation. Show them you are interested, but don't be pushy. Discuss a variety of topics in detail during this critical step:

- Child care responsibilities
- Housekeeping responsibilities, if any
- Work schedule- hours and days
- Nanny's experience and background
- Overtime
- Car usage
- Personalities and lifestyles
- Children's health problems, if any
- Child rearing philosophies
- Living arrangements and rules, if live-in nanny
- Pay, benefits and payroll taxes
- Background checks

Try to take short notes, but don't look down on your note pad all the time. It is crucial to maintain good eye contact. You can ask for a copy of the job description if the family had typed up one. If not, listen to them carefully and see if there is something you don't like. Try to get a feeling of the household and how things are done. One of the most important things is the child care philosophies of the parents. If there is something that you can not adapt or like, this should be a concern for you when you make your decision.

Choosing the best match for you

Everyone has a way of doing things. Every parent has a way of disciplining their children, feeding them, choosing activities for them to participate and so on. Face-to-face interview is the time to discuss all these and determine if this family is a good match for you. You can not agree with everything, but the important thing is how big the differences are. A good nanny is adaptable, but that doesn't mean that you have to change yourself completely to get the job. If there are big differences in discipline and child rearing philosophies, it is best to move on to the next interview. If there are minor differences and you think you can adjust to their way, great. Be careful not to have too many of these little things also. When you put them all together, they can amount to a big problem.

Remember a good match is the most important thing for you. You want to keep a job at least for a year. If you realize a mismatch occurred after you start, you'll have to start looking all over again. No one likes countless job interviews. Stability is not only good for the children, but also for the nanny. It takes time and effort to get settled in a new job. Children need to warm up to you, you need to get used to the household routine. It is all time consuming and you want to avoid going through that too many times.

Listen to your instincts and use common sense. Examine the job description carefully and determine if the job is within your capabilities. Interview will tell you a lot about the family and their lifestyle. Observe the interaction between the children and the parents to see if your discipline and child care philosophies differ greatly. Talk about these in detail, down to the children's diet. If you are a health conscious nanny and the parents feed their children junk food, you may want to move on to the next family in your list. Be smart and ask as many questions as you like. Avoid repetitive and redundant questions. Listen to the answers carefully and take notes. Interview all the families you are interested in even if you think you have found your dream job.

Be picky and choosy. If you are a good nanny, you will have no trouble finding a job that fits you. Present yourself well and understand what the job entitles. You will have a pretty good idea if a family is right for you after the interview.

Background checks

Nowadays, nanny background checks have become an integral part of the recruiting process. It would be ideal if people would not have to do criminal checks on the nanny candidates; however, it would be foolish to think so. After all, it is the parents' responsibility to make sure their children are with a nanny who has a clean record. If a family states that they would like to have a background check on you do not get offended. It is at a family's best interest to perform a background check on a nanny who will take care of their most precious possessions. Parents can have a peace of mind just by performing some or all of the common nanny background checks. You will need to give a signed release authorizing the background check. This is required as the background checks can not be done without your consent. Below are the most widely used nanny background checks:

27

Social Security Number Trace

Social security number trace will verify that the number given is indeed a valid social security number and belongs to you. It will also report your known aliases and your addresses for the past seven years. This is the first and most important step of a successful nanny background check process. It is considered a good practice to first check your social security number and your name given to make sure they are accurate and match.

County Criminal Records Search

As the name applies, county criminal records search is done for one specific county. If you lived in more than one county, a separate search may be done for each county you have lived in. Although the information differs from county to county, most counties provide both misdemeanor and felony convictions dating back seven years.

Motor Vehicle Records Search

This is extremely important if the nanny is expected to drive the children around. DUI's and speeding tickets can make the parents think twice. If you will be driving the children around, a clean driving record is crucial. Clean record proves that you are a responsible driver and probably are a responsible person in other areas as well. It is recommended that you obtain a copy of your driving record from the local DMV office as some states do not release these records to a third party. The cost to obtain it is usually very low and you can use it for all the families you are interviewing.

Sex Offender Registry Check

Each state keeps a sex offender database. This search can be done at the state level and a national database is being built as well. If a nanny candidate has lived in more than one state, separate search must be conducted for each of the states she has lived in the past.

<u>Your references</u>

References are a big part of getting a nanny job. This is the turning point on making decisions for almost all families. Previous employers make the best of references. That's why it is important that you leave each job in good terms. This is an industry where references can make all the difference. Written references can be asked before leaving a job, but are not really enough. Almost everyone would prefer to talk to a person on the phone as they can get a better feeling about the reference and ask whatever questions they may have.

Make sure that people who are your references have a good impression of you and are ready to give excellent reviews. It is considered a nice gesture for your past employers to talk to the people they don't know so that you can get a job. They are not obligated; be careful not to be a burden on them. It is hard for a mother with children to be tied up on the phone. You don't want every family you interview to talk to your references and cause a burnout on them. It could be damaging to your relation with the family as well. References should be checked only when a family is almost ready to hire you. The best time for them to do this is after the interview, not before. Although some families may want to talk to your references before a face-to-face interview, you should at least have a feeling that you are a strong candidate for the job. Explain the reason to the families you interview with. Tell them that you are interviewing several families and do not want this to be a burden on your past employers.

Organize and notify your references before giving the names to the parents. Make sure to call all the references you will be using to get their permission so that they can be ready. Parents are impressed with excellent references; an old employer who says wonderful things about you gives them a reassurance.

New nannies always struggle with the fact that they don't have adequate child care related references. Keep in mind that you can use the families you babysat for, clergy, and teachers. Only references that are not appropriate are your family members, relatives and friends. Generally, these connections do not make professional references.

Check references of the family

Families check your references and perform background checks on you. Shouldn't you have a way to check with the past nannies of the family? You have every right to do so. As a matter of fact, you must be as thorough as the families before accepting a job offer. Ask the family to give you the names and phone numbers of their previous nannies or babysitters. Call these references only if the job prospect is good. Just like you, family is probably interviewing several candidates and it wouldn't be fair for every candidate to call the past nannies of the family.

Choose your questions prior to the phone call. Keep a note pad and a pen to take notes. Ask open ended questions and wait for them to answer. Most people would expect yes or no questions; however, those questions won't give you any additional information you are trying to get. Make sure the person relates to you and is comfortable talking with you. Do not call right before dinner or early in the morning. It is best to arrange a time slot if you feel that you called at an inappropriate time at the first try. You don't want to rush this crucial part of the job search.

CHAPTER 3 - STARTING THE JOB

You found the perfect job and you are anxious to start. New jobs bring excitement and, naturally, hesitation. You need to start from scratch to build a new relationship and prove yourself to your employer. You hope they like you and the children will have a smooth transition. You wonder if the children will warm up to you easily; especially if they have just said goodbye to a nanny whom they liked very much or they changed several nannies recently.

Start period of a job is a critical time. There might be so many things to remember that you may feel overwhelmed. You may feel insecure about your abilities if the job setting, duties and the children's age group are all new to you. If you have moved from another town, there might be the added stress of moving a new area and homesickness. These are all temporary and common issues that go away with time. The important thing is to hang in there and do your best.

Work agreement

Importance of signing a work agreement can not be emphasized enough. This document can be your safety net to protect you from misunderstandings. With everything written down and signed by both parties, there is not much room left for errors. That's why when you get a final job offer a solid nanny employment contract is needed. This document is usually created by the employers; however, it is your responsibility to read it thoroughly before signing it. It should, at a minimum, clearly state the work schedule, hours, duties, pay, pay frequency, taxes, overtime, car usage, vacation, and benefits. If the position is live-in, items about this arrangement should be incorporated into the agreement. Some of the things to include for a live in situation are accommodations, curfews, privacy, rules about having guests in the house, and phone usage.

A well-written work agreement is an essential document, but the more important thing is to follow it. This applies to both the nanny and the family. If changes or additions to the agreement are needed in the future, they must be done mutually and both parties must agree.

Items to be included in a nanny work agreement:

- Start date of employment
- Work days and hours
- Overtime
- Responsibilities
- Pay
- Pay frequency
- Sick days
- Vacation
- Holidays
- Taxes
- Insurances
- Auto usage
- Mileage reimbursement, if nanny's car is used for the job
- Performance reviews
- Pay increases
- Confidentiality
- Termination
- Signature of both parties

Additional items for live-in nannies:

- Accommodations (room and board)
- Phone usage
- Guests
- Privacy
- Curfews

Trial period

How can you be sure you picked the right job? There is no way to guarantee everything will be just fine even if you were very thorough with your job search. Things may seem different when you start the job. What if you told the family that you would commit to a year at least when you accepted the job offer and it turns out that this job is not really for you? That's why a number of people set a trial period before committing to a long term commitment. Nanny agencies usually have this condition as well. The first month is the trial period where both parties get to know each other and see if they are a good match. If everyone involved knows that the first month is a trial period, then it is easier to call it quits if things don't work out the way they like.

You should receive your agreed salary during the trial period. Stay away from any family who tell you otherwise. You are still working and this is not a period for a family to get free labor. Trial period certainly is not meant to be used to fill the gaps in employment or child care. It is the beginning of a job; you are there for the longer term unless something really bothers you about the job. Most families and nannies stay together after the trial period. Unless there is a major disagreement or misunderstanding, chances are you will too.

Orientation

New job and responsibilities can be overwhelming at times. Transition period can be stressful and confusing for all. This is the time where your organizational skills can be most useful. No matter what kind of job you start, there should be always someone showing you around to help you get acquainted with the routine. This is especially important with the nanny jobs as you will be working in someone's house and need to know where everything you need is.

A full or half day of orientation to get things moving is sufficient in most cases. One of the parents usually stays with the nanny on her first day on the job to help her out. With infants and toddlers, there is really no one who can help you find things are around the house. School-age children are more helpful; they have a pretty good idea where their things are and what their routine is like. In any case, do not solely rely on the children to help you with these matters. It should be the parents' responsibility to make sure you have everything you need on the first days.

You will also need to get yourself familiar with the neighborhood and area. It is always a good idea to meet the neighbors, especially the ones closest to the house. This may become crucial if you have an emergency. Drive around the area to locate the grocery store, convenience store, gas station, library, ice cream shop etc. If you need to drive the children to the school or regular activities, determine whether you can find your way around. If not, take a ride with one of the parents to learn the routes. This is the best time to learn your way around, not when you are alone in the car with a car full of screaming children. Try to memorize the address and the phone number of the house. You may need these for a number of reasons and will eventually memorize them at some point. The sooner you learn them, the better.

Try to absorb as much information as you can when you have one of the parents around. Pay attention to how the parents discipline the children. This is a great opportunity to learn the job and make the transition smooth for everyone. Take notes or ask the parent to write down some of the important things such as medical conditions and emergency contact numbers. Just like any other job, you will feel more comfortable when you are faced with the job alone if you have the information you may need at hand.

Things to do and have before taking charge
The first day alone with the children in an unfamiliar environment can be scary. Skilled nannies are confident, yet they are not afraid to call up the parents when in doubt. Parents will expect your phone calls on your first week and be happy to answer your questions as long as they are not too often and redundant.

You must have the following at hand the minute you take charge:

Emergency phone number list:
- Local emergency, poison control and local police
- Parents' phone numbers at work with their direct extension numbers
- Parents' cell phone and/or beeper numbers
- Pediatrician for each child along with the office address
- Dentist for each child along with the office address
- Neighbors and emergency contact relatives

Medical Consent Form
Medical consent form allows you to authorize emergency medical and dental care for a child. In case of an emergency, you may have to take a child to the hospital and the child may need emergency care. Every nanny should have a medical consent release form in case one of the

parents can not be reached and the child needs emergency medical treatment. You can then authorize the medical or dental procedures the child needs. This form should include the parents' names and phone numbers, child's information including blood type, medications, allergies, social security number, doctor's and dentist's contact information, and the medical insurance information. The form must be notarized and must be kept in a place where you can easily locate if needed. It is not uncommon for some nannies to carry one in their car or purse.

Calendar of activities

Parents like their children to participate in various activities. Most of them are fun and beneficial to children's development. They keep children busy and help them improve their social skills. Nowadays, there are even activities for infants and toddlers. You may come across a toddler with a full schedule ranging from playgroups to swimming lessons. Some parents tend to register their children of any age in multiple activities and some children's schedules may even confuse an experienced nanny. With multiple children, things may get hectic and it could be nearly impossible to remember everyone's schedule. If you feel that you can not keep all the activity schedules in your mind, ask the parents to give you a calendar of activities. Most parents mark these on the kitchen calendar, but have it in a format that you can easily understand what is going on.

Directions

Most nannies drive children around in their own car or in a car provided by the family. You might be great with directions, but everyone can get confused when there are too many directions to remember. This is especially true at the beginning of a new job. It is always a good idea to ask the parents to write down the directions to the places you need to drive. Grocery stores and places around the neighborhood might be easy to remember. However, it is always a good idea to have addresses and directions for the playgroups etc. written down.

First Aid Kit

Generally, every house with children has a first aid kit ready. If there is one when you start the job you must make sure it has everything you may need or learn the location of it. Check the contents periodically and make sure the used items get replaced right away. First aid kit must include everything you may need to treat cuts, allergies, and other minor emergencies. There are several prepackaged first aid kits on the market. It is always wise to keep an extra kit in the car that you transport the children in.

Bonding with the children

Children eventually warm up to people who are loving and kind to them. Creative and nurturing nannies should be able to bond with most children sooner or later. First days or weeks can be tough; children can miss their parents or old nanny.

Using your creativity may come in handy in this situation more than ever. Children are easily distracted. Find out about their favorite activities and games. Invite children to play their favorite games with you. They will like the fact that you have something in common and before you know it you may be his new best friend. Naturally, this can be hard to accomplish if you are in charge of more than one child. Children love attention and compete for the attention of the adults around them. If this is the case, you may want to spend few hours alone with each child while you have one of the parents around. On your orientation day, you can spend some quality time with one child while the parent is watching the other child.

It is a well-known fact that children are not thrilled about having a new person in the house to take care of them. Children like stability and they need it. Change in child care is always a stressful event in their lives. It could also be stressful for you provided that children will be more moody the first few days and perhaps openly tell you they do not want you around. Some children act up when their parents are around and change as soon as their parents leave. Bonding with the new nanny will take longer than a day or two. At the end, children like kind and nurturing people. Treat them with respect and you will see the results faster.

Working with a work-at-home parent
Most nannies don't like to work with a work-at-home parent. They would not even interview for such job. This setup is particularly difficult to deal with and inconvenient for any nanny unless the parent's office has total isolation from the house and she or he is not on your way. Problems with this situation start with children banging on the parent's office door for attention. No child will let his parent just close the door and do his work. This may not necessarily be the case with older children, but no toddler will agree to this. He knows this mom is home and think that she is ignoring him. This causes more resentment and tantrums. You will have a child who is furious almost all day. Even older children can be unmanageable; they may want to run to their mom's office when nanny declares homework time. These scenarios may sound outrageous, but common even if you are taking care of the best-behaved children in the world.

The next problem will be related to the parent at home. Most work-at-home parents will be tired of listening to cries and screams at their door. Eventually, they will be frustrated and perhaps blame you for it. They will think you are not capable of keeping the children out of her sight. Parent will be angry as well due to the fact that she can not get work done. Parent may also give into some of the requests of the child just for the sake of getting some work done. This will cause a fall out between you and the parent as the discipline styles will clash. Children must be disciplined in a consistent manner by all adults in their lives. When inconsistencies surface, children get mixed messages and it will get rough down the road.

The best setting for this arrangement is to keep the children out of the house as much as possible. Take the children on long walks, go to the library. Fill most of the day with activities outside of the house so that the children are not preoccupied with thoughts such as "mom is home and she does not want to play with me". Otherwise, this arrangement seldom works and experienced nannies do not even put themselves in such a stressful environment.

CHAPTER 4 - LIVE-IN NANNY

As the name implies a live-in nanny lives with the family in their house. Some stay for five days and go to her house on the weekends while others live with the family everyday of the week. Live-in nannies are provided with a free private bedroom and board along with a salary. Although a nanny may have reservations about living with her employers, this arrangement can be very beneficial. Housing savings can amount to a fortune in some metropolitan areas. Family does not charge you for rent, utilities or food. You get all these as a perk of the job even though your salary might be little less than of live-out nannies' in the area. If you had just moved to a new town, you have the parents to ask questions and perhaps introduce you to new friends. You won't have to spend countless hours looking for a place to live or free time to get the utilities connected. Living with the family can save time, money and effort. It can also help you build your social life. Any nanny can be a live-in nanny provided that the job is a live-in position. However, one should keep in mind that a live-in nanny does not leave and go to her house after work. She lives with the family in their house. This arrangement may not suit a nanny who desires her total privacy of her own home after work, but may be ideal for others.

Most families pay live-in and live-out nannies almost the same amount. However, generally live-in nannies get paid a little less. It is unacceptable for a family to calculate how much the nanny would pay for room and board if she had lived outside and deduct the amount from her wages. Families should realize that having a live-in nanny has its

40

great benefits for them and should be paid a fair wage just like a live-out nanny. It doesn't cost the family much extra money to provide a room and board for the live-in nanny.

Typically live-in nanny arrangement best suits parents who work long hours, irregular schedules, travel for business or commute long hours. Nowadays, many other families who work regular 9 to 5 jobs like to hire live-in nannies as well. With a live-in nanny, parents would never have to worry about nanny arriving on time or arriving at all in the morning. She lives right there and takes her only a minute to get to work! Sick days or bad weather would not be big concerns as the nanny would not have to drive to work.

Accommodations

A live-in nanny must have her own furnished private bedroom. If a private bedroom can not be provided, live-in nanny option should be crossed out. In addition, the nanny room must be furnished adequately. Bed, bed linens, desk, chair and lamp are just about the bare necessities to make the room comfortable. Extras such as TV sets, DVD players and CD players make the room a better sanctuary; however, lack of them is no reason to turn down a job. They can be found at most stores and the prices are more affordable than ever. If not, most families would allow you to use theirs. You should make sure your room, at least, has the necessities to live in it. Some families take this very seriously and turn the nannies room in to a five-star hotel room. If they can't, it does not necessarily mean they don't care. Some people just may not have the decorating touch and may leave it up to you to turn your room in to your own.

Most families provide a private bathroom or a bathroom shared with children. A private bathroom is desirable for the sake of privacy, but most houses may not be equipped for this arrangement. If you are sharing a bathroom with a child, you may need to schedule your showers/baths around his.

Separate living quarters sometimes called "nanny quarters" or "in-law suits" is ideal for maximum privacy. Newer houses may have this separate area, some with private entrance and even a kitchen. This arrangement works out the best in terms of total privacy.

Needless to say, it is your responsibility to keep your own living areas clean. If a maintenance issue arises it is also your responsibility to notify the parents about it. Even though your own area should be off limits to the family, maintenance crews should have easy access to it when needed.

Food is provided by the family no matter who does the grocery shopping. Most live-in nannies eat meals with the families and/or children; some may follow a special diet and prepare her meals separately. How to handle the dinner time should be discussed during the interview. Most families welcome their nanny to eat dinner with them. Keep in mind that this is just about the only quality time most families spend together and may want to be alone. There is nothing to be offended if this is the case. Be sensitive and objective to their needs. If they want to enjoy the dinner time as a family every day or some days, it's within their right. Some nannies even like not to eat dinner with the family and use this time as down time. Eating a quiet meal without any distractions can be a soothing way to start the evening.

There is also the nanny who only eats specific food and wants to prepare her own meals. Parents should still provide the food within a reasonable limit. Some special diet foods cost significantly higher, in this case family may expect you to buy some or all of your food, e.g. organic produce etc. If the family does not buy organic food for the household, they will object to buying it for you. If the differences are small, there should not be problems. For example, you may like orange juice rather than apple juice or cantaloupe instead of watermelon. These differences are not really so big in terms of cost. Always keep in mind that your eating habits play a big role in the children's eating habits. Eat healthy around the children so that they will grow up to be healthy eaters. Remember they copy your behavior, good and bad.

Relocation- homesickness

Most live-in nannies are young women who had just moved to a new area. Moving itself is a stressful event. Adding the anxiety of a new job and living with your employers on top of it can send your stress level to upper limits. Remember that you must always try to put on your best face when working with children. They can sense stress and they are already under stress because of a new adult in their lives. If you keep a positive attitude, you will settle and start enjoying your new life faster.

There will be an adjustment period for you to make new friends and familiarize yourself with a new town. Naturally, you may get homesick and miss your family and friends back home. This is even more true so for a nanny who has never lived away from home before. It is a big step for a young person to move away from home. You may be in need of new friends to meet up on the weekends or to have coffee after a long day of work. Everyone needs the same and you may be surprised to find out that there are other people around in the same situation. If you live in an area where there are a lot of nannies, you are in luck. This is the best place to start. Finding other nannies would be the best thing to help you and your charges with your social circle. Children can play together and you can have someone who is in the same profession as you. She may even have other nanny friends she can introduce you if she has been in the area for a while.

Parents can also give you a helping hand meeting new people and exploring the new area. As a matter of fact, they should take you on a tour of the area on your orientation day and as needed within reasonable limits. This is especially important if you will be driving the children. No one should just type up the directions and expect you to drive all over a new town. Knowing your way around the roads would make you a confident and better driver. Sometimes it may be hard for others to understand how it feels to move to a new town and not know anybody. Busy parents may not realize that as they have their plates full with full time jobs and children. Under any circumstances you should find ways to make new friends to make your transition an easy one.

Privacy

Privacy is usually the biggest concern in a live-in arrangement. Both parties have to give up little from their privacy in order to coexist in the same house. Both sides have to compromise to make this situation work, but the rewards can be well worth it. It is not uncommon to see many live-in nannies become a member of the family. Out-of-town nannies can appreciate the newly found family more than anyone and turn out to be happier than they would if they had lived on their own.

Live-in arrangement may take some time to get used to, especially for nannies who have never worked as a live-in nanny before. This is very normal; as long as everyone respects each other's privacy, living with a family you like can be emotionally supportive and fun. The downsides can be the common issues which can be found in any family setting and you probably had to face such issues in your parent's house as well. Hanging out around the house in your pajamas on the weekends will become a thing of the past. You may hear arguments you do not want to hear. You may unintentionally hear or see confidential and private information about the family. Naturally, a professional nanny would keep such information to herself and not talk to anyone about private family matters.

Phone usage

Acceptable telephone usage during work hours and off hours must be discussed during the job interview. Most families do not complain about one or two daily phone calls as long as they are short in duration. However, personal phone calls must be avoided during work hours. Any responsible nanny would know not to spend too much time on the phone as children need constant supervision and the phone can be distracting.

Out-of-town nanny may need to make significant amount of long distance calls if she gets homesick. It is advisable that she does them during her off hours and pay for her long distance calls when the phone bill arrives. Phone cards may become very handy if you want to avoid all the hassle of calculating your portion of the phone bill. You can buy a prepaid phone card which can be found in most grocery stores and use it when needed. Of course, the family may not like their phone line to be tied up as they need to use it as well. In this case, a separate phone line to your room or a cell phone might be a good solution for everyone. Most cell phone companies offer free weekend minutes that can be used for long distance calls as well. Nowadays, some parents provide their nannies with a cell phone for emergencies and pay the monthly bill or put the phone in their family plan. In this case, parents should be responsible for the monthly phone bill. Nanny pays for the personal calls in excess of the phone plan.

Car usage

Most live-in nannies may not own a car and rely on a family car to not only transport the children but also for their personal use. In this case, an acceptable usage policy must be discussed and agreed upon by both parties. Naturally, parents should realize that the nanny needs to have a social life and friends, especially if she is new in town. If you drive a car provided by your employers, they are responsible for all the expenses and upkeep of their car; however, you would be expected to pay for gas for your personal trips. Parents may also want to put a limit on how much you can drive their car for your personal use. For example, you might be expected not to take their car out of state. They may also put a mileage limit that you should not exceed every week or month. They would also expect you to keep the car clean and notify them of any maintenance issues such as oil change or any other problems that needs attention. Family should put you on their car insurance right away and pay for it as well. You may be expected to keep the car with a full tank of gas, but it should be paid by the parents.

If you are driving your own car to transport the children to school, playground, activities, playgroups, shopping, and anywhere else they need to go, you should be compensated for mileage rather than just the cost gas. The reason for this is to make up for the wear and tear of the car and other related expenses such as maintenance and insurance which is paid by you.

Current mileage rate is $0.45 per mile per IRS, but it may change. Check with IRS to find out what the current rate is. Keep a mileage log to avoid any misunderstandings or mistakes. Mileage log could be a little notebook that you can list the daily trips at the end of the day. Family doesn't pay for any other car related expenses if you are compensated for the mileage. You would be responsible for the gas, maintenance and insurance. You get reimbursed $0.45 per mile for each mile you drive for the children. This also applies to the miles you may drive for family's errands and such.

No one wants to think about problems, but you should be well-aware of what can go wrong and how to handle them. This includes car accidents if you would be driving. Having a car accident can be costly; always practice safe driving to avoid accidents. No matter whose car it is if the nanny is at fault at the accident, it is natural to expect for her to pay for the deductible. If the deductible is a big amount, family and the nanny can share the cost of the deductible. However, having an accident of a fault of your own itself can put a dent in the relationship. If you can afford it, you might as well pay for the whole deductible. Sometimes you may find yourself stuck with a deductible even though you have nothing to do with the damage in the car. Examples of this would be a hit and run while the car is parked in the library parking lot. In this case, family should pay the deductible whether it is their car or not due to the fact that you are out for the children. Discuss all these scenarios with the family before taking the job. Have these conditions spelled out in your work agreement to cover any unpleasant surprises.

Parents must provide the nanny car seats for each child regardless of whose car she is driving. Car seats must be appropriate for the children's age groups. Children must be restrained in their car seats at all times while driving. Nanny is expected to ensure that children are safely and properly buckled in their car seats as well as obeying all the traffic rules.

House rules, overnight guests, visitors, curfew

A live-in nanny is entitled to her social life during her off hours. Parents would want their nanny to have fun and unwind to prevent burnout. Keep in mind that you should abide by the house rules, especially during the work nights. If you decide to go out at night, you must let the family know when you will be back. It is common courtesy to let the people whom you share a house with know your whereabouts. You can have car trouble or any other problems while you are out and it is for your own safety to let the parents know when you will be coming home. There might also be an alarm system in the house or a dog that may bark and wake everyone up.

Family may set some rules for overnight guests of the nanny. Families like to be notified ahead of time about overnight guests nanny may have. Parents should keep in mind that nanny needs a life of her own outside her job and respect her privacy as well. However, it is bad taste to invite boyfriends to stay over and most parents would object to that. Remember you are a role model for their children. Whatever you do outside their house should not be their concern as long as it doesn't affect your job performance. You may have friends who might come over to visit you during your off hours. Your living area should be off limits to the family, but that does not mean that you can bring anyone to the house particularly as an overnight guest. Most parents would not object to your close relatives staying with you as long as it does not interfere with your job.

Setting a curfew for an adult may not seem appropriate, but it should be discussed during the interview. There is a reasonable hour during work days that everyone should be in to get enough rest for the next work day. If a nanny wants to stay out late during the work nights, lack of sleep may even pose a safety hazard for everyone around. You must always be alert while watching the children and proper rest is the key to that.

Boundaries- blurry schedules

Sometimes the work hours and duties of a live-in nanny may get a little blurry. This is a sensitive area. Parents should be extra careful to stick with the schedule and duties outlined at the work agreement. If the parents are running late, nanny should be notified and paid overtime for the extra hours worked whether she is live-in or not. You too need to unwind during your off hours since you spend the entire day at work as well. Most nannies take their job very seriously and work very hard. Their days are long and they need be alert at all times to keep the children safe. Therefore, they have to get their rest and time off to recharge.

Speak up if you feel your schedule and duties are getting overwhelming. Do not bottle it up as it only leads to resentment. Parents should understand you work hard too and appreciate it. If they are constantly running late or asking you to do extra chores, it is time to bring these up in the weekly meeting. Families do not like to lose a good nanny; they would rather work around the problems to keep you.

How to live together successfully

A nanny work agreement is necessary to spell out the living arrangements and rules. Having this piece of paper may eliminate big problems in the future. Once in a while, there will be issues and disagreements even between the best of families and nannies. Keeping the communication lines open is a key element in a good nanny-parent relationship. Issues that bother either party should be discussed in a civilized manner and resolved without wasting any time. Be a good listener and expect the same. Listening to others in an objective manner is a great gift and a quality of a great nanny. It is the best form of respect one can show to others. Once the person across you sees that, he or she will respect you even more. This even applies to the children you take care of.

Waiting for the problem to go away does not work and causes more problems to pile up. If you do not air a problem that has been bothering you, other little things will start to irritate you and turn in to a snowball effect. As long as you bring up matters in a respectful manner, parents will appreciate your courage and professionalism. Weekly meetings are a great way for the nanny and parents to sit down together and review any issues that may come up during the week. These meetings also allow you to spend some alone time with the parents to get to know one another better.

Prevent burnout

Being a nanny can be an isolated and exhausting job. Unfortunately, not many people realize that. All hardworking nannies are well-aware of this and resent people who think the opposite. Mental and physical requirements of the job can easily burn out even the best nanny who does not take care of herself. Take care of yourself well so that you can take care of the children. This includes healthy eating, appropriate rest and exercise for your physical well-being. Your off hours are yours whether you live with the family or not. Do things that make you happy when you are off work. Make friends and maintain your friendships for your emotional health.

Some nannies state that even taking a sick day off can be troublesome when living with employers. It may seem simply impossible to "call in sick". Keep in mind that even a super nanny would need her rest when she has the flu. It is also for the children's best interest that you do not come in contact with them if you are sick. Parents should have a back up plan even if you live in their house. This could be calling a relative or a babysitter or one of the parents staying home for the day to take care of the children.

Sometimes people feel burned out even if there is nothing wrong with their job. This may stem from working at the same job for a long time or being a nanny for many years. If you feel that you want to try a different career, you might need to quit your job to pursue other interests. Most working parents would understand and even relate to your dilemma. Plan well before you decide to quit your job.

CHAPTER 5 – COMMUNICATION

Constructive communication is an essential part of every relationship. Marriage, work and anything else that requires human interaction thrive on healthy communication. This is even more true so for a nanny-parent team who commit to work together to raise healthy, happy children. Daily interaction between the caregivers is a crucial part of the children's development. Keeping one another abreast of the children's physical, mental and emotional development daily helps with the transition of the roles every day.

Good communication can be achieved with both parties' willingness and dedication to resolve issues at hand. Most of us feel that bringing up problems to our employers can be a scary thought due to the fact that we fear their reaction. We may not feel comfortable or simply do not know how to approach or put our concerns into right words. We worry about hurting other's feelings or putting a dent in our relationship. What if I get fired for bringing that up? What if they don't like me anymore? As a result, most people keep the problems bottled up to avoid the anxiety which can lead to more serious problems.

In order to master the art of effective communication, one must posses certain interpersonal skills. Those skills can be learned or improved through experience and effort. Needless to say, a great nanny is the one who works tirelessly on her child care and interpersonal skills to better herself. Being a nanny is a very unique job like no other and involves constant human interaction. You would not only need to understand the needs and feelings of the children, but also their parents as well.

Listening

Effective listening skills are the first steps to successful communication. True listening requires work on the part of the listener, concentration and interaction. It is not as easy as it sounds. Our minds are constantly working; intentionally or unintentionally. We need to empty our minds as much as we can to listen effectively. We need to concentrate to actually process the words we hear. We need to start putting the whole picture together in our minds without being judgmental and empathize with the speaker. Our body language, the way we sit and nod are all indicative of our eagerness, or lack of it, to listen and really understand others. How do we listen genuinely to actually hear and understand what the other party is saying?

Focus on the speaker. Empty your mind and concentrate on the speaker. Try to turn off the noise and chatter in your head. Do not preoccupy yourself on how you will respond in turn. Not paying full attention to the speaker is a form of disrespect.

Maintain good eye contact. Eyes connect you with the speaker and express your feelings and reactions. Do not try to hide your feelings, but avoid intimidating the speaker. Speaker needs to feel comfortable as well to get his or her point across.

Maintain a relaxed body posture. Your body posture can be an indicator of your receptiveness. In turn, speaker will be willing to share more. Sit in a relaxed and calm manner at an appropriate distance from the speaker. Do not invade personal space. Look relaxed and focused with a soft facial expression.

Acknowledge. Understand what is said and acknowledge when you do. This could be in a way of briefly repeating the speaker or simply by nodding. Nodding is the preferred method of acknowledgement because you don't confuse the speaker by interrupting verbally.

Do not interrupt. Speaker needs to concentrate to express herself or himself clearly. If interrupted often, she or he may lose the control of the flow of his or her thoughts. Try not to interrupt except when you don't understand something and need to ask the person to repeat what he or she has said.

Think before react

Knee jerk reactions don't bring productive results. Think before you speak, always. Tell the speaker you need some time to think if you need to take a few minutes. Take a moment to pull your thoughts together and concentrate on the situation at hand. Person across you should appreciate the fact that you are taking the time to organize your input and hopefully come up with an effective plan.

Empathize with the speaker. Put yourself in his shoes. Try to see where he is coming from. Keep an open mind and try to really understand the speaker's point. Determine if the person has a valid point or he or she is blowing things out of proportion.

Don't only remember bad things. Most of us remember negative past experiences and get into a defensive mode when faced with problems. Our brains start bombarding us with negative thoughts such as "I don't deserve this" "I am not appreciated", blocking us to focus on a positive solution for the problem.

Concentrate on the problem at hand. Don't be distracted by past experiences. Don't try to compare past circumstances with the current one. Every issue and the elements surrounding it are different from each another. Approach the problem at hand and concentrate only on it.

Don't be judgmental. People have different opinions of different things or people. Most of them have something to do with the way we are raised and taught. Don't try to categorize people or try to find common characteristics between your past employers and current ones. You will miss the whole point if you get sidetracked with such things. Everyone is an individual and everyone deserves a chance.

Focus on a positive solution. Think of a positive solution and how you can be a part of this solution. This should be your only concern when working out problems. Be positive and it will reflect on your creativity to find solutions.

Talking- Bringing up problems

Art of communication is best used when you need to bring up problems. This is a very sensitive area. Whether your employer is the one who initiated the conversation or not, some simple guidelines can produce the best results to achieve the goals.

Always start your speech with positives. Point out the positive aspects of your job; mention how well the children are doing developmentally or how grateful you are about being able to take that afternoon off when your parents were in town visiting. Remind them that you respect them for working hard and raising great children. Parents need to hear these from time to time as well as you do. Why not give them a pad on the shoulder like you would expect them to do to you?

Be articulate. Be clear in your thoughts and how you express them. Explain your feelings and worries. This will help others better understand where you are coming from and empathize with you.

Don't use "you" statements. They sound accusatory, threatening and may cause others to get angry. Instead of saying "You did this", use "I" or "we" statements. Talk about your feelings; say "I feel that the children might be getting mixed messages regarding discipline." instead of "You are confusing the children by telling them it is okay to drink soda.".

Do not be emotional. Don't be defensive. People do not regard defensive people as credible. Some people see it as a sign of weakness or guilt. Put feelings aside, concentrate on the facts pertaining to the issue at hand. Review the facts and come up with a plan to resolve the issue. Do not let your emotions get on your way of seeing the facts.

Be sensitive to other's feelings. Do not be critical. This goes hand in hand with being defensive. Criticizing is the next step for people who are defensive. Do not try to prove who is right and who is wrong. Instead work on the problem constructively.

Bring up creative solutions. Think of the ways to resolve the problem. Be open-minded, creative and flexible on the solutions. Formulate few solutions for every problem if you can to give everyone some options. If not, ask your employer to come up with his or her solutions and setup a time to discuss the matter further later on. You do not have to resolve everything on one meeting. That's nearly impossible to accomplish as most solutions are working progress. It is an important achievement if the problem is identified and understood by everyone at the first meeting.

Nanny/parent relationship

It is imperative that a good rapport between the nanny and the parents is established from the very beginning. For a successful relationship nanny and parents should work hand to hand. Both parties should agree on discipline and other childrearing issues from the very beginning and reinforce each other's behavior towards the children. If the children get different messages from their nanny and parents, problems may arise for everyone. Nannies should follow the parent's advice on how to raise and discipline the children. However, if there are major disagreements, it should be discovered during the interview process. It is hard to imagine a health conscious nanny to survive in a household where potato chips are breakfast food.

Nannies and parents should never lose sight of the fact that they are a team. The primary goal of this partnership is the well-being and healthy development of the children. Both parties must do their best for the good care of the children and discuss the issues in a civilized and respectful manner. Every relationship needs work and maintenance. Open communication and respect are the first steps to an honest, working relationship.

Communicating with children

- Children start to understand words as early as six months. That means they start understanding what is said to them long before they can talk. Talk to them, read books and tell them stories no matter how young they are.

- Be respectful no matter how young the child is. You are his role model and he will copy your behavior and manners. He will treat you back the same way.

- Give your undivided attention when they speak. They can sense when they are not heard as they look up to you for feedback, praise, encouragement, approval, or disapproval.

- Speak to them in a kind, gentle, nurturing and loving tone. They need to feel they are loved more than adults do. Choose your words wisely. Never say anything hurtful no matter how your day is going. If you are feeling under the weather or impatient on a particular day, catch your breath for a minute while the child is occupied.

- Listen patiently. Don't get impatient or angry no matter how long it takes the child to express his thoughts and feelings. Never raise your voice in frustration.

- Children are sensitive. Be extra careful not to hurt their feelings in any way. Ask them what the matter is if you feel like something is bothering them.

- Use correct grammar instead of baby talk.

- Explain the rules and the reasons behind them in a way that they can understand. Do not make untrue or unrealistic statements. These will only confuse a child.

- Do as you say. Keep your promises. Never promise a child something you can not keep. Be a positive role model.

- Do not criticize the child. Encourage him and build his self-esteem through your actions and words.

- Avoid power struggles. This is a common issue with toddlers than any other age group. Drop unimportant matters to avoid arguments. Do not push the child to do something he doesn't want to do unless it is important such as taking medicine.

- Do not talk about adult matters in front of children.

- Do not talk about the children or their parents in front of the children.

Employment agreement

It is foolish to start any job without signing a well-drawn employment agreement. Being a nanny is a serious job and careful consideration should be given to what the job involves and the conditions. Appropriate documentation should be prepared and agreed by both parties. Agreement is prepared by the employer. You should read it thoroughly before signing and point out any parts you do not understand or disagree. Remember what you have discussed during the interview and make sure everything that is important for you is written down. A good employment agreement clearly states the work days, hours, pay, benefits, duties, and vacation time. These are the critical elements for you to protect yourself from future misunderstandings.

Daily logs

Daily log is an important tool to keep track of the children's development. It is especially important when caring for an infant. Older children can communicate their needs or what they ate during the day when parents ask. With an infant, parents have no way of telling how much formula or milk the child consumed when they were at work. You might be giving a verbal summary when they arrive in the evening, but people tend to forget things after a long day of work. They usually won't feel comfortable about calling you at home in the middle of the night to ask you why the baby is cranky. Instead, you can use a notepad to take notes about medications, how much the child ate, when he ate, how many times he had a bowel movement and anything else related to the children. Parents looking over the notes can easily figure out the baby is cranky because he might be constipated or hungry. Parents can take over the care smoothly using the log and even write down anything you would need to know on the log while you are not there.

Weekly meetings
A weekly or monthly meeting can help both parties bring up issues. It is also beneficial to keep track of the children's development. Most parents overlook this due to hectic schedules and assumption that everything is going smoothly. They don't want to sit through another meeting after a day full of meetings at work. Only after the nanny suddenly quits they realize there were actual problems that they were not even aware of. This goes both ways, not all employers are good communicators. They too may bottle things up and end up letting go a nanny instead of spending an hour a week to discuss matters.

Every relationship requires work. Nanny-parent relation is no exception to that. Weekly meetings can be the only opportunity to air any issues and praise the work well-done. These meetings do not have to be about issues or problems only. Positive aspects can be celebrated. Everyone needs a pad in the back, this includes the parents. It is okay for anyone to show appreciation to each other. Actually, it is necessary. Most people think that the other party feels how much their work is appreciated; however, everyone needs to hear it once in a while.

Inform the parents of their children's physical, emotional and mental development during the meeting. Give them reasons to be proud of their children and see you really do a great job. Always start and end the meeting on a positive note. Do not forget to talk about both positives and negatives. This way everyone knows relationship is on the right track and can be improved even for better.

Performance reviews

Performance reviews are an excellent way to reevaluate things. You get to reevaluate your job, determine if you want to continue working for the same family or move on to new challenges. Parents evaluate your performance and probably offer you a raise or bonus for a job well-done. Performance evaluation is completed by the family and given you for your review. Then, time is set for discussion. You may take down notes as you read the evaluation and bring up your input during the discussion.

Handle criticism objectively. Do not be emotional if everything is not great. Honesty is better than insincerity and takes a lot of guts. Learning about your shortcomings or skills can help you improve yourself even more. This is a good opportunity for your professional development. Keep the evaluations for your future jobs to use as a reference. Prospective families would admire your openness and seriousness about your job.

CHAPTER 6 - LEAVING THE JOB

No matter how perfect everything has been at your job, there comes a time when one of the parties decides it is time to part. This could be initiated by you or the parents. You may simply feel that you need new challenges or a change of scenery. You may prefer working with certain age groups and your charges are way past those age groups. Some nannies feel more comfortable with infants while some prefer school-age children. It is your professional life and you are in charge of it. You should do the best for yourself as well as the family you are working for.

Burnout factor is felt by many nannies. Taking care of children physically, being alert and creative requires a lot of energy on nanny's part. It is common for a nanny to seek complete change of scenery and perhaps move to a different profession. A good employer will not try to stop you if you wish to try new things in life. Most genuine families will be happy for you.

Sometimes, you may feel that you are growing apart with the parents or even with the children as they get older. There is a lot of emotions involved with this type of job and feelings sometimes overtake the facts. Pay attention to your feelings and the facts at hand. If you feel that it is time to move on, do not try to place blame on anyone. Show effort to make the separation easy on everyone involved.

When terminated by employer

If you are a career nanny and worked for several families this may have already happened to you. Remember it is harder on the person who is suggesting to part. Assuming that the reason is natural, such as family moving to another town or children starting school full time, you should be given a few weeks notice. Depending on the length of your work with them and your closeness to the family, it is not uncommon to see a month's notice and severance pay. Two weeks is usually not a realistic time frame to find a new job. You may not be able to find a job which starts on the exact date that your current job ends. Severance pay is a great way to offer a helping hand for you to get back on track again.

If you are in parting in good terms, hopefully you are, have an exit interview. It can be particularly beneficial to your career and professional development. People learn by feedback and end of a job can teach you a lot about where your skills are. When you search for your new job you would be better equipped with this knowledge. You would find out the areas that can be improved and work on them.

Quitting gracefully

Quitting a job is never easy, especially in a job where friendship is most likely to occur. It adds extra stress and sense of insecurity if you are not sure of your plans ahead. Parents feel the same if you are the one leaving the job unexpectedly. To make things easier on everyone you can do two things. First and most important one is to give enough notice for parents to find a good replacement. Ideally, parents would like you to even train the new person.

Remember to never announce your decision in front of the children first. Have a meeting with the parents and explain what is going on when the children are not in the same room. Parents may have their own strategy to tell the children any news that directly effect to them. Discuss with the parents how and when to tell the children. Next step is to prepare the children for your departure. This is where you actively involve. Make sure the children understand that your decision has nothing to do with them. Tell them you will visit and do visit soon after you leave. Call them on the phone, acknowledge their birthdays and drop by to say hello every now and then. Try not to overdo it as children need to get used to not having you around everyday. If they have a new nanny, it is not appropriate to call or show up to a degree where the new nanny is uncomfortable. She needs to settle and take over. You can slowly decrease the number of visits and calls as the children get used to the new setting.

CHAPTER 7 - CHILD DEVELOPMENT

Each child develops at his own rate and pace. No two children are the same and they will not develop at the same pace. A child may develop at a faster rate than his peers in some areas while he may be lagging behind in other areas. It is not uncommon to see a baby walk faster than other infants at his age, but talk later than his peers. An infant may concentrate on walking first and start walking as early as nine months. Same child may start talking later than his peers. Children concentrate and put their efforts into one developmental milestone at a time. That's why the pediatricians leave a wide time frame for the milestones. They don't start worrying about developmental problems before that time window passes.

Nurturing child care plays a tremendous role in a child's physical, mental, social, and emotional development. This applies from the birth all the way into the young adulthood. Children flourish in a safe and loving environment which allows them to explore the world on their own. As a caregiver, it is a nanny's to duty to provide a loving, safe and active environment for her charges no matter how old they are.

Infant
Infants are dependent on their caregivers more than any other age group. Feeding, bathing, dressing, diaper changing and all other vital needs are met by their caregivers. They are helpless otherwise. Infants are well aware of this and this is the time they need to develop a sense

of trust. They need to know they will be well taken care of and their needs will be met promptly. They need to know they will be fed by their primary caregivers when they get hungry, their diapers will be changed when wet and they will be soothed when they have gas. Some parents worry about spoiling the infant by picking him up every time he cries. It is not really possible to spoil a baby at the early months of infanthood. Although some parents decide not to pick up a crying infant to let him "cry it out", this is the only way infant can communicate. He will cry out loud if there is something bothering him or if he merely wants to be held. Caregivers should respond to his cry to help develop his sense of security. Babies, especially newborns, like cuddling and being held close as it simulates the womb. Trying to adjust to the outside world is not easy for newborns and they like anything that reminds them their mother's womb.

Physical development- Babies sleep as much as they need during first months. After the first three months, most babies start taking naps; one in the morning and one in the afternoon. Sleep hours start to decrease; however, some may start sleeping through the night after the first three months.

Newborns need to be fed as often as every few hours. Experts agree on the benefits of breastfeeding the first year of life. Infants who can not be breastfed drink formula the first twelve months as cow's milk should be avoided the first year. Most babies are ready for solid food between four to six months. Baby cereal is usually the first starter solid food. If the baby is ready for solids, he will enjoy the new taste along with breast milk or formula. Soft fruits and vegetables, such as pureed banana and squash, can be introduced one at a time to monitor any food allergies. By the time infant turns twelve months, he can eat several finger foods and feed himself sitting on a high chair.

Muscle control and motor skills develop from head to toe. Young infant can turn his head side to side at the early months, but can not hold his head up. His head must always be supported when picking him up. He slowly gains control of his head at the early months. Grasping objects starts around three months. Around seven or eight months, most babies can sit without support. Even though infants may have strong legs earlier, most babies start walking between nine to fifteen months. At around nine months, most can hold small objects between thumb and fingers.

Newborns are nearsighted. They can see a distance of twelve inches. This is the distance between the baby and the caregiver during bottle feeding or breastfeeding with the mother. He can follow your face with his eyes if you move your head back and forth slowly. His sight improves as the visual pathways of the brain mature. Infants start hearing sounds at the womb- mother's heartbeat, voices, and sounds. They can start hearing and responding to sounds by turning their heads to the direction of the sound source. They may not understand what is said at the early months, but a baby can start understanding speech as early as six months. That is one of the reasons why talking, signing and reading to the children regardless of age is so important.

Cognitive development- Verbal interaction is essential for infant's mental development. This is a crucial period for brain development. Baby's brain is still developing and he is absorbing everything around him. Don't give up because the results are not seen right away at the early months. They are learning and building up information for future use.

Emotional development- The most important goal of this stage is to build trust. This is the backbone of the baby's future emotional health. Infants need to feel safe and secure. They have the need to develop sense of security with the important adults in their lives.

Infants start showing emotions such as delight and distress in the early months. They start smiling at parents and caregiver. They love being cuddled and develop attachments, generally to their mother. Close to the end of the first year, fear of strangers develops.

Toddler

Often associated with temper tantrums and stubbornness, this stage of a child's life is the period when exploration and curiosity is at its peak. Most children start to walk and explore by now. This new-found freedom enables them to approach anything in sight and grab anything within reach. Needless to say, the first thing comes to mind is to provide a safe and secure environment for toddler to explore. He can flourish in a safe environment and satisfy his curiosity about all the new things that he did not know existed before.

Physical development- He is walking by now without help. This is the time to childproof the house. Most toddlers also talk some words, phrases or short sentences, but usually not enough to clearly express himself. This is also one of the causes of the frustration. Most toddlers cut down to one nap, skipping the morning nap. Eating slows down worrying most parents. Physical growth slows down compared to the first year and appetite decreases. He can participate at the family dinner as he can use a spoon and sit on his own in high chair. Most are capable of bladder and bowel control; however, may not be ready for potty training. Readiness for potty training takes more than just physical capability.

Cognitive development- This is a very important time for the mental development of the child. Toddler is ready to be introduced to many new things that he did not know existed before. This includes just about everything. He will want to explore his immediate surroundings, starting with the house, first. His curiosity must be supported and

67

encouraged for his healthy mental development. He can only flourish if caregivers allow him to explore and learn. He may get frustrated at times if he can not figure out something. He may appreciate a helping hand as long as he is in control. Although he is becoming independent he still needs adult guidance and can follow simple directions. It is the adult's responsibility to provide an environment where child makes the best of his curiosity and learn as much as he can.

Emotional development- Temper tantrums are generally ever present. He is still socially immature and enjoys physical affection. He is self-centered and has limited concept of others. Stubbornness is also a characteristic of this stage. Everyone, at some point in life, has met a toddler at the grocery store yelling "no" at the top of his lungs. By now, he has formed an attachment to his mother and gets very upset when separated from her. Support and encouragement at this stage will help the child form self-esteem and assurance.

Preschool
Around the ages of three and four, children start to develop more social skills by playing with their peers. Playmates can teach each other how to form friendships and start to become an important part of a preschooler's routine. Active play with his peers improves his skills of cooperation and imagination. A safe and supervised environment must be provided for him to learn how to play with other children, learn to share toys and make friends.

Physical development- By now, most children are equipped with the motor skills to play and explore the world. Most can draw simple objects on paper, ride a tricycle, throw a ball and run well. Toilet training, a major milestone, is accomplished at this stage by majority of children. Feeding is independent as he can feed himself without help now, can use a spoon and even a fork. He can start to dress himself starting with putting on his shoes although can not tie the shoe laces early at this stage.

Cognitive development- Talking improves, graduating from short sentences to full sentences around age four. Three-year-old will question everything around him, usually in the form of "why" questions. Endless questions may become cumbersome to adults, but do your best answering. He is curious about the world surrounding him. Ability to talk opens up new doors of communication; he can tell simple stories. He wants to understand the world better and is highly imaginative. Imaginary friends usually appear at age four.

Emotional development- Children of this stage enjoy the company of other children. Playmates are essential for the social growth of the preschooler. Preschool is a great way to encourage social life and emotional development. If preschool is not an option, small playgroups would serve the purpose. Starting with one playmate and short periods of play time, child can learn sharing and cooperative play. Children may parallel play at the beginning and move on to play together. Parallel play is more beneficial than playing alone as the children may still need to share toys and communicate with each other; children are still getting something out of the experience just by being around each other. Children should always be closely supervised and helped at this critical stage where they turn into more social beings. They can flourish their social skills by the encouragement and help of their caregivers. Children who master play dates can graduate to group games around age four. Separation anxiety is overcome at this stage and the child gains the skills he needs to start the school.

School-age

School-age children are social beings; they like being around other children and play cooperatively. This is also the time where they get involved in sports. Group sports with rules; such as baseball, can help them learn how to follow rules in a structured game while being a part of a team. Organized sports are a great outlet for children to have fun and learn at the same time in addition to providing much needed physical exercise.

Physical development- Motor skills are fully mature by now. Handedness is established by age five. They are physically ready to play most sports; it is advised to start with the safe and simple ones. They may have a particular interest or skill set for a specific sport and should be encouraged in that direction without pushing too hard. They like responsibilities and following rules. They can do chores around the house and should be encouraged. Starting with simple chores, they can graduate to more complex chores to be self-sufficient adults in the future.

Cognitive development- Most children have a firm grasp of language by age five. Pronunciation is fully matured although some children can have trouble with some sounds early on. This is usually temporary; however, caregivers should keep a close eye on the progress and possible problems. Although vocabulary usually improves throughout the years, school-age children have sufficient vocabulary to tell long stories and they enjoy it. Sentence structure improves over the years; by the age of nine he can talk much like an adult. Listening, memory, attention span, and following directions improve greatly. They master reading and writing along with other subjects during these years.

Emotional development- Children of this age are self-assured, cooperative and well-adjusted. Social life is a big part of their life now. They love being part of a group and want to feel competent in it. They are trying to establish a separate identity within the group as they get ready to step into the adolescence years. School-age children still need adult guidance on social manners. Role models are very important at this stage where they start to learn social skills and develop empathy for others.

Adolescent

This is the period where child learns to establish his identity. Importance of role models is vital as he relates to them while searching his own identity. Lack of good role models may cause identity crises which may result in delinquency and rebellion. Adolescence stage is often associated with rebellion even with well-adjusted children. Body goes through major changes as womanhood/manhood is established. These changes alone are enough to confuse an adolescent. Strong role models and adult guidance are needed, perhaps more than ever, at this stage while the child tries to gain his independence.

Physical development- Bodily changes are visible and may cause confusion without proper adult support. The body is transferring from a child's to a man/woman's. Explanations before the changes happen are the best way to prepare the child to what is going to happen. Establishing an open line of communication can also help the child open up if there is something bothering him or if he has any questions about the changes going on with his body.

Cognitive development- Adolescent can think abstractly. They start to develop their moral code, which is why good role models are necessary. Only through open and honest communication with his role models the child can establish his beliefs and values. Communication is a two way street. He needs to be heard when he talks. He then can figure out his identity.

Emotional development- Most adolescents go through a moody and introspective period by the age of sixteen. Opinions of others, especially his peers, are at most importance during this time. He tries to fit in with his peers while demanding more privacy at home. He starts to pull away from his parents as tries to establish independence.

CHAPTER 8 - SAFETY

Children of all ages are immensely curious. Their curiosity is an important element of learning and should be encouraged. They will only learn by exploring the world around them more and more. It is the responsibility of adults to provide a safe environment for the well-being of the children. Young children's environment must be child-proof. Anything that can pose a danger to the child's health and well-being should be removed from the environment. As soon as the child starts crawling, he will try to reach anywhere and anything he can. This is the time all safety hazards within his reach must be removed. This includes any room he is allowed in. Although most parents put up child gates to divide the areas to prevent the baby crawling everywhere he wants to such as up the stairs, all rooms must be evaluated in the house for safety. It is not uncommon to take an infant to a room with you not to leave him alone even if the house is child-proofed. He can be practically anywhere and injure himself especially if the room is not properly child-proofed.

Baby Safety

Head- Babies are fragile and should be handled gently. This is especially important on the first few months of baby's life. He has no head control in the early months and can not hold his head up on his own. Young infants' heads should always be fully supported through the neck when picking up and holding him.

Most babies have two soft spots on their heads; one on top of the head and the other one little behind it. These areas should be handled very carefully and gently. Bones in these areas are not fully developed and are still growing. Rear spot usually closes by four months and the front by the first birthday.

Delicacy of a baby's head can not be emphasized enough. Even a little shake can damage a baby's brains. Babies should never be shaken, even lightly. It may cause permanent brain damage or even death. Always keep in mind before touching a baby that they are fragile.

Umbilical cord- Newborns umbilical cord should be quite dry within the first few days. This area should be kept particularly clean to prevent infection. Diapers should be folded over in order to keep the area dry; otherwise soaked diaper can get the area wet with urine.

Crib and sleep- Babies must always sleep in a crib that is in excellent condition and meets the current safety standards. Crib should be placed away from any windows, curtains, draperies, blinds, or anything else with long cords in order to prevent infant reaching those items. Never put a baby down to sleep on a beanbag, waterbed, sofa cushion, pillow or adult bed. Infants can suffocate on such surfaces. In addition:

- Mattress should fit snugly in the crib
- Mattress should be firm
- Do not place a pillow in the crib
- Use a soft, lightweight baby blanket in the crib
- Always place the baby on his back in the crib to prevent SIDS
- Sheets should fit the mattress and wrap around the corners
- Bumper pads should be securely attached around the entire crib

- Bumper pads and mobiles should be removed when infant can pull himself to standing position
- Do not attach a pacifier around baby's neck with a string
- Keep all toys out of the crib when infant is in crib

Diaper change- Infants' diapers must be changed quite often whether they are dirty or not. Newborns can easily go through twelve diapers a day. Here are some important safety pointers about diaper change:

- Always wash your hands before and after changing a diaper
- If using a changing table, never turn your back on the baby or leave a baby alone on the changing table
- Always buckle the belts if using a changing table
- Place all the supplies you need to change the diaper within your reach beforehand
- Keep the supplies out of baby's reach
- Prepare a clean and warm area to change the baby
- Wipe baby girls front to back to prevent urinary tract infection
- Apply ointment if there is diaper rash
- Dispose dirty diapers immediately

Feeding- Babies drink formula or breast milk first year of their lives instead of cow's milk. Breast milk is recommended by experts; if not an option, infant can be bottle-fed formula. Infants also start solid foods between fourth and sixth month. Cleanliness goes hand to hand with bottle feeding. Newborn's bottles must be sterilized between uses and formula always must be kept fresh. Some important safety points when feeding babies are outlined below:

- Do not feed an infant under twelve-month-old cow's milk

- Do not heat bottles in the microwave
- Test temperature of formula/milk on your skin before feeding the infant
- Feed baby in an upright position
- Do not prop the bottle on baby
- Remove air bubbles from bottle
- Always burp baby after feeding
- Never reheat or reuse leftover formula
- Sterilize bottles newborns use
- Never give hard food to an infant

High chair- High chairs are great help to feed a baby or toddler efficiently and safely when used properly. There are several health and safety hazards associated if not used accordingly. Important safety issues related to high chairs are:

- Always use the safety straps, buckle both waist and crotch restraints
- Food tray alone will not prevent babies from slipping
- Never leave a baby alone or unattended on a high chair
- Do not let child stand on a high chair
- Do not keep the high chair close to the table, counters, wall, or windows with blinds/curtains

Crawling/cruising toddler- Once a child starts crawling, he will want to explore everything he can reach. His environment must be free of safety hazards for a safe learning environment. Entire house must be child-proofed and the best way to go about it is to get on all fours to see what baby is seeing. Common household dangers exist almost on all houses; here is the list and what to do about them:

76

- Cover all sharp corners with edge protectors, especially coffee tables
- Remove all cords within his reach; blinds, electrical cords, and phone cords
- Cover all electrical outlets
- Lock all kitchen cabinets within his reach with latches
- Lock all cabinets within his reach with cleaning supplies and dangerous materials
- Place nonskid strips under the rugs; this should be done when baby is born or before
- Remove house plants from floors
- Remove dangling table clothes
- Remove unstable furniture or secure them on the wall; e.g. TV stands, book shelves
- Install child gates on the stairways
- Store knives and sharp objects out of child's sight and reach
- Try to use the back burners of the stove; if you use the front burners, turn pan handles toward the back
- Do not use a mobile baby walker

Car Safety

Children of all ages must be properly restrained in age-appropriate car seats when driving. This is the law and starts with bringing the baby home from the hospital. Car seats should be in top condition; never use a car seat that has been involved in a crash. Older models of car seats may also lack today's safety features and should not be used. Car seats must be installed in the car according to the manufacturer's instructions. This goes for the car and the car seat or booster seat. Unfortunately, most are not properly installed and pose a safety hazard.

Local fire department can be a great help in this critical issue. Things to pay attention when it comes to car safety:

- Never leave a child unattended in or around a car
- Infants should be in a rear facing infant seat until 12 months and 20 pounds
- Children who are over one-year-old and 20 pounds can use a front facing car seat until they are 40 pounds
- Children over 40 pounds can use a booster seat until the age of eight
- Car's seat belts should not be used for children under 80 pounds and 4 feet 9 inches tall
- All children under twelve years of age must ride in the back seat of a car
- Always wear your own seat belt to set an example and for your own safety
- Keep a first aid kit in the car or bag
- If children cry or distract you while driving, pull over to a safe place when you can to tend their needs

Water Safety

Water accounts for several accidents and deaths each year. Bathrooms and bath time pose an everyday risk. The first step to prevent any accidents is to child-proof the bathroom. All sharp objects; such as razors, should be placed out of child's sight and reach. This goes for medicines and cleaning supplies as well. Appliances such as hairdryers should never be kept or used around water. Bathroom floors get wet and should be covered with non-slippery rugs to prevent falls. Summer season is especially dangerous with outdoor activities, especially pools. Even if a child knows how to swim he should never be alone in a pool. Many people rely on lifeguards in public pools; however, you are the one responsible for the child's well-being. Do not leave any buckets with water around the house; children are known to drown in less than an inch of water.

Bathing
- Never leave a child unattended in the bathroom
- Water heater in the house should be set to 120 F
- Bathtub should be outfitted with a non-slippery rubber bath mat
- Never answer the door or phone while bathing a child
- Place all the bath supplies within your reach beforehand
- Never leave the water running in the bathtub while the child is in it
- Do not place the child near the faucet
- For infants, fill the bathtub only up to two to three inches of water
- For young children, do not fill the bathtub higher than child's waist when sitting
- Bathwater should be warm between 96 F and 100 F
- Use a baby bathtub for newborns and appropriate bath seat for infants
- Baby bath seats can tip over, never leave the child unsupervised in them

Pool
- Never leave a child unattended around the pool
- Always use sunscreen and reapply it according to the directions on the package
- Always watch the children around the pool regardless of their capability to swim
- Children should not run around the pool; it can cause slips, falls and injury

- Keep a cordless phone around the pool
- In-house pools must have fence and a gate with self-closing and self-latching mechanism
- In-house pools should be covered when no one is using them and completely uncovered when swimming
- Babies should only go in the baby pool and must be held at all times in the pool
- Babies must wear waterproof diapers in the pool
- Keep babies away from drains in the pool
- Older children should never dive where it is not specifically marked for diving
- Learn CPR

Choking

Choking and suffocation are among the leading accidents with young children. Most ordinary items around the house can be a dangerous threat to a child just starting to walk. When child-proofing the house such items must be put away to prevent accidents. Choking can be caused by food that is not suitable for the young child or toys with small pieces. Bottle feeding should be done properly to prevent infant choking. Children should always play with age-appropriate toys and the toys should be evaluated before and during use.

It is essential to know what to do if the child starts choking at least until help is on its way. Even though you may never need to perform CPR on a child, it does not hurt to be trained in infant and child CPR. To prevent choking:

- Do not prop bottle on a baby
- Make sure the child is in upright position when eating
- Do not feed a young child hard handy, popcorn, hotdogs, raisins, or nuts

- Cut children's food into small bite-size pieces
- Feed infants only soft solid food; baby cereal, pureed soft vegetables and fruits are okay
- Do not perform Heimlich Maneuver on infants
- If an infant is chocking, turn him over along your arm securely and pat between the shoulder blades
- Do not let child run around with food in his mouth
- Do not let children eat in the car while driving; you won't be able to interfere if something goes wrong
- Plastic bags, coins, balloons, buttons, and toys with small parts should be out of reach to prevent suffocation
- Keep dangling cords out of reach
- Do not put a pacifier on a string around a child's neck

Fire Safety & Burns

Fire is the leading cause of household death in the United States. The main reason of death is not the flames, but the smoke inhalation. It is essential to educate children about fire and be prepared when it comes to fire safety. Fire drills should be practiced often and children should be actively involved. Visits to the local fire house are always fun for kids. They can learn more about the seriousness of fires and how to be safe during these visits. Here are a few things about fire safety:

- Smoke detectors must be installed and checked periodically in the house
- Keep matches, lighters, and chemicals out of children's reach
- Do not overload electrical sockets
- Do not run electrical cords under rugs or furniture
- Unplug small appliances after use and keep them out of children's reach

- Keep a fire extinguisher on each floor in the house and learn how to use it
- Keep a special fire escape ladder for the second floor and learn how to use it
- Teach children fire safety and talk to them about the dangers of fire
- Have a fire escape plan out of the house
- Have fire drills once a month
- Keep the hot water heater in the house at 120 F to prevent burns
- Keep children away from hot water, hot pans, stoves, and ovens
- Make sure children wear only flame-retardant sleepwear
- Radiators, fireplaces, and electrical heating devices must be screened
- Dryer vent must be cleaned of lint after each drying session

Bicycle Safety

Riding a bicycle is a part of childhood and great exercise if done right. Each year thousands of children end up in the emergency room due to bike related accidents. Most unfortunate accidents are head injuries and can be deadly. Head is the most important part of the body to protect when riding a bicycle; safety helmets must be worn properly to prevent injury to the head. Some safety measures must be taken and children should be taught how to ride their bicycles safely:

- Children must always wear a helmet when riding a bike
- Helmet must fit the child's head and straps must be fastened
- Always watch and supervise children when riding
- Do not allow children ride on the road or driveway
- Bicycles should be maintained and all parts must be kept in good working condition

- Wearing bright colors and putting reflectors on the bike allows others to see a child on the bike better
- Shoe laces and loose pants legs should be avoided on the bike
- Children should never ride their bicycles barefoot

Food Safety

Safe handling of food is the most important step to prevent food borne illnesses caused by bacteria such as E. coli and Salmonella. Food safety starts with buying the food at the grocery store. Strict rules must be followed during shopping, storing and preparing as well as storing the leftovers. Importance of hand washing before, during and after food preparation can not be emphasized enough. Before preparing any food, wash your hands with soap and warm water for 20 seconds. Repeat it during preparation as many times as you need.

Grocery shopping & storing

- Do not buy canned food if the can looks dented or damaged
- Do not buy fruit with broken skin; bacteria can enter the broken skin
- Do not buy meat, poultry, or fish that smells out of the ordinary
- Do not buy juice or cider that is not pasteurized
- Always check expiration date of food when purchasing
- Beware of servings when reading ingredients on the package
- Always wash and dry the cans before opening canned food
- Drive home and refrigerate perishables right after shopping, especially on hot days
- Fresh vegetables, fruits and dairy products last about one week in the fridge

- Make sure juices of the chicken and meat do not contaminate other food. Keep and store them in separate durable bags or containers to prevent cross contamination.
- Refrigerated meat, poultry and fish should be consumed within two days
- Store eggs in the refrigerator shelf in original carton, not in the fridge door

Preparing food
- Always wash hands thoroughly with hot water and soap before preparing food and after handling raw meat, poultry, fish, and eggs
- Scrub fruits and vegetables under running water to clean pesticides and chemicals
- Keep raw meats, poultry, fish, and eggs completely separate from other food during preparation. Do not let their juices run into anything. Thoroughly clean and wash everything that comes in contact with them. This includes cooking utensils, cutting boards, countertops, pots, pans, and plates.
- Always thaw raw meat, poultry and fish in the refrigerator, not on the counter top
- Cook eggs thoroughly before serving
- Do not serve anything that contains raw eggs including cookie dough
- Do not keep eggs in the room temperature more than two hours
- Use a meat thermometer when cooking raw meat; cook poultry up to at least 180 F and hamburgers 160 F
- Place leftovers in a shallow container and refrigerate within two hours of cooking
- Thoroughly reheat leftovers before serving
- Consume leftovers within three days of cooking
- Sanitize the kitchen wipes and dish towels often

- Wipe countertop and stove after food preparation
- Keep kitchen floors clean; clean up food spill immediately

CHAPTER 9 - EMERGENCIES & FIRST AID & CPR

Keeping children safe and well is a nanny's primary responsibility. Constant supervision and providing a safe environment are essential to keep young children out of trouble. It is always a possibility that you may find yourself in an emergency situation and must be prepared for it. Being calm is as important as knowing what to do in case of an emergency. Should you encounter an emergency, you must pull yourself together and calmly apply your knowledge depending on the type of emergency.

You may come across an emergency where a child may need medical attention. Always have a list of the emergency phone numbers including the numbers for the pediatricians, dentists, hospital, poison control, and local emergency services. Keep the emergency numbers in a visible place around the house. Most people post them on the refrigerator. Learn the location of the nearest hospital and the directions to get there. Some people naturally panic during emergencies; it doesn't hurt to have the directions written on a piece of paper.

Every family you work for should provide you with a Medical Consent Form for you to be able to allow medical personnel to treat a child if needed. This form should spell out the parent's name and contact information as hospitals will try to contact the parents first. If they can not locate the parents, you can allow medical treatment on the child. Detailed insurance information and child's medical history including illnesses, medications, allergies, immunizations and blood type should all be clearly spelled out on this form. Parents fill out the form and sign it in front of a notary public before handing it to you. Make sure it is done properly and has all the vital information before you need to use it.

First Aid

Below you will find some general information about emergency situations and what to do about them. American Red Cross offers First Aid courses throughout the United States. Every child care professional should be trained in first aid and have a first aid kit handy as it is very possible to come across an emergency while taking care of children.

First Aid Kit- Keep a well-stocked first aid kit in the house and the car. Prepackaged first aid kits can be found in drug stores and come loaded with most of the necessities; however, you may want to customize your kit for your charges' special needs.

Every well-stocked first aid kit must contain the following items:

- sterile gauze
- adhesive bandages in different sizes
- adhesive tape
- elastic bandages
- antiseptic wipes
- cotton swabs
- sterile dressing
- hydrogen peroxide
- acetaminophen and ibuprofen
- hydrocortisone cream, calamine lotion and antibiotic creams
- Pedialyte and/or Infalyte

- tweezers
- safety pins
- scissors
- ice pack
- thermometer
- eye patch
- arm sling
- tongue depressor
- flashlight and extra batteries
- plastic gloves

Animal bites- Animal bites are preventable. Children should be taught not to touch stray animals and must be supervised at all times when interacting with house pets. Minor scratches can be cleaned with soap and water; however, medical attention is needed if the bite has punctured and broken the skin. Keep an eye on the scratches and seek medical attention if the area turns red, swollen and painful. Stray and wild animal bites; such as foxes, raccoons, bats, skunks, can cause rabies and child may need shots. Report any stray animals to the local animal control.

Broken bones- Broken bones caused by falls are common among young children. That is why prevention, childproofing the house and constant supervision, is very important. Swelling, bruising, tenderness, tingling feeling around the area are all symptoms of a broken bone. If you suspect child has a broken bone seek medical care, call 9-1-1 or local emergency number to take the child to the hospital. If the injury is in the head, neck or back area, do not move the child to prevent further damage. If the bone is sticking out, do not move the child or do not try to stick the bone in. Keep him lying down until the help arrives.

Burns- Hot liquids and household appliances are the common causes for burns in small children. Appliances should be out of children's reach; small appliances should be unplugged after use. Children should be kept out of the kitchen when cooking. Handles of the pots and pans should be turned toward the back burners if you must use the front burners.

First degree burns are caused by brief contact with heat. Redness, pain and dryness are characteristics of this type of burn. Treatment can be done at home by running cool water over the effected area. Gently apply a gauze bandage. Do not apply ice on the burn.
Second and third degree burns must be treated by a health care professional. Call the emergency number right away.

Choking- Choking on a piece of food is quite common among young children. Most of the time, the child can cough and recover. If the child can not talk or cough and he is turning blue, you should intervene right away. For older children you should perform Heimlich Maneuver. This should not be performed on infants under one year of age. They require a different technique. If an infant is choking, lay the baby face down along your forearm, support her head and shoulders and give 5 sharp slaps between her shoulder blades. CPR training is essential to apply these life-saving techniques correctly.

Cuts- Minor cuts can be treated at home; deep cuts or cuts that don't stop bleeding require medical attention by a health care professional. If the child has a minor cut, rinse the cut with water and apply pressure over it using a sterile gauze or clean cloth. Change it when it is soaked with blood. Raise the body part to minimize bleeding and cover it with bandage after the bleeding stops.

If the cut is deep or you can not stop the bleeding, seek medical care right away. Call your local emergency number for help.

Dehydration- Diarrhea, fever, vomiting and intense physical activity on hot days are main causes of dehydration. Dehydration caused by diarrhea is a leading cause of death among infants worldwide. Dehydration may also sneak up on a child without an obvious problem. If a child is playing outdoors for long hours on a hot summer day, he may loose water through sweating. The lost fluid must be replaced periodically by drinking water throughout the day regardless of child's thirst. If you wait until child is thirsty, he might already be dehydrated. If the fluid is not placed, the child may become dehydrated. Common signs of dehydration are:

- Fatigue, dizziness and lightheadedness
- Cool, dry skin
- Dry mouth
- Decrease in urine output- less than six wet diapers a day for infants and eight or more hours without urination for older children
- Few or no tears when crying
- Sunken fontanels in infants
- Sunken eyes

Treatment for dehydration is to replace the lost fluids. For older children, if dehydration is mild and caused by excessive sweat, let the child drink as much water as he wants. After the first few hours, he would also need food or drinks that contain sugar and salt (electrolytes). Keep the child in a cool place and let him rest.

If mild dehydration is caused by vomiting or diarrhea, unless advised otherwise by the pediatrician, oral rehydration fluids should be given slowly to rehydrate the child instead of just plain water. Most of these are available at the drug stores and can be purchased without a prescription. Try to give the solution slowly, one teaspoon every few minutes. Avoid salty broths, water, soda, ginger ale, tea, fruit juice, gelatin desserts, chicken broth, or sports drinks.

Child should be rehydrated over the course of few hours. Once dehydration is over, child can resume his regular diet. If the child does not improve or the dehydration is severe, you may need to take him to the emergency room. Health care professionals can give the rehydration solution through the vein, in the form of IV, which is more effective.

Drowning- Young children may drown even in an inch of water. Although pools and lakes are very dangerous, buckets and bathtubs with water can pose a drowning risk to any child as well. If you come across a child who is drowning, get him out of the water immediately. Call the emergency number and start CPR if necessary.

Electrical injury- Electrical outlets and cords pose danger to children if not covered or placed out of sight. Children can get electrical shock by sticking objects into electrical outlets or chewing on the electrical cords.

If a child is injured, disconnect the power supply. Remove the child from the source of electricity with a nonmetallic object; wooden objects are the best. Seek medical attention as electrical shock can cause internal damage to the body. Child must be examined by a doctor after the accident to make sure his internal organs are not affected.

Falls- Falls are very common among young children and mostly result in small bruises. If a child suffers a mild fall, apply ice pack on the bruise and let the child rest for a while. You should keep the child under observation for the next 24 hours to notice any changes. If you see any changes that worry you, seek medical attention.

If the child is unconscious or injured this head, neck, back, hipbone or thighs, you should not move the child. Instead, you should call the emergency services right away. If you suspect that child is having difficulty breathing or not breathing at all, you may need to start CPR after you call for help.

Fever- Fever is the body's way to fight with germs. Body sets its temperature to a higher degree in response to an infection, illness or another problem. Our normal body temperature should be around 98.6 F although it may slightly differ throughout the day and depending on the activity. In older children temperature of and under 102 F usually does not pose a risk if the child can carry on with his normal activities and there are no visible problems. In newborns, up to 3 months of age, a rectal temperature of and over 100.4 can pose a serious problem and emergency care should be sought.

You can take the temperature of a child using a digital or mercury thermometer. Mercury thermometers are considered old-fashioned and can pollute the environment if not disposed properly. When it is time to dispose one, it should not be just thrown in the trash. Nowadays, digital thermometers are very common and usually very accurate. Due to their easy use and popularity, they are sold widely at the drug and grocery stores.

Temperature can be taken rectally, orally, and auxiliary. With infants and young children who are not able to hold the thermometer in their mouth or under their arm, it is best to use the rectal method. Make sure this thermometer is only used for rectal temperature taking. Some type of water-soluble lubricating jelly is first applied to the tip of the thermometer before inserting it in the rectum. Insert it between half an inch and one inch. Stop inserting it if you feel resistance. Hold the thermometer and keep the child calm until you hear the signal indicated on the user's manual that the thermometer is ready to be read. Always read the instructions on the package before using a thermometer or ask a doctor.

Older children can use the oral or auxiliary method if they can hold the thermometer long enough. Ask the child to hold the thermometer under his tongue or under his armpit. Take the child's shirt off when using the armpit method; thermometer must touch the skin directly for an accurate reading.

Most fevers are treated by giving the child acetaminophen or ibuprofen to relieve his discomfort. If the child has an infection or another problem, these fever reducers will not cure the problem. They only provide temporary relief so that the child is not irritable. You can also try giving the child sponge bath in lukewarm water. The water should not be cold or hot; rubbing alcohol or ice packs should be avoided. Child would also need plenty of fluids to prevent dehydration as fever causes loss of fluids faster. Give the child water, soup and non-caffeinated drinks. Last but not least, make sure the child gets plenty of rest.

Head injury- Risk of head injuries can be greatly reduced by wearing protective head gear when riding a bike, playing sports, or skating. Even though most head injuries are minor, medical attention is almost always needed with any type of head injury. If the injury is very minor and the child seems to be acting normal, you should observe the child for the next few hours for any changes. Application of ice pack can help the minor bumps and bruises. Do not directly apply ice; wrap in a clean towel. Do not apply pressure in case of a skull fracture.

If the child loses consciousness, becomes dizzy, vomits frequently, complains of pain, has a seizure, or has any other noticeable change and discomfort, he might have suffered an internal injury. In this case, seek medical attention and call the emergency services right away. Do not move him if you suspect a neck or spine injury.

Heat exhaustion- When it comes to heat-related illnesses, young children and elderly are at the highest risk. Hot summer months can be extremely dangerous to young children who participate in strenuous activity like outdoor play for long periods of time. Children who play outside during summer days should be properly hydrated. Light-weight and light-colored loose clothing is also advised. The best time to be outdoors on hot days is the early hours of the morning or late hours of the afternoon. Shady areas, like a big tree or patio cover, can also block the direct sun exposure and help child feel cooler. Heat exhaustion is a mild illness; it can strike children who have been playing outside on high temperatures and have not been getting enough fluids.

Symptoms of heat exhaustion are:
- Dehydration
- Heavy sweating
- Clammy skin
- Weakness
- Dizziness
- Fatigue
- Irritability
- Muscle cramps

- Nausea/vomiting
- Hyperventilation
- Headache
- Fainting

If not treated, heat exhaustion can escalate to heat stroke, which is a serious illness. To treat heat exhaustion:

- Bring the child to a cool and shady environment
- Remove the child's clothing
- Give the child water and food
- Give the child a bath with cool water; do not use cold water
- Have the child rest

If the child does not feel better in the next hour or the symptoms worsen, seek medical attention.

Heat stroke- Heat stroke is a life-threatening medical emergency. The body loses its ability to regulate its temperature and can rise up to 106 F. Sweating mechanism shuts down and the body can not bring down its temperature. If not treated by medical personnel, heat stroke can be deadly or can lead to severe disability. Call emergency services immediately if you see these symptoms:

- High body temperature- above 105 F
- Hot, dry, red skin- no sweating
- Unconsciousness
- Throbbing headache
- Seizure
- Fatigue
- Weakness, dizziness, confusion, or nausea

If you suspect child is having a heat stroke, bring him inside while waiting for help to arrive. Remove his clothes and sponge him with cool water. Do not give him any fluids. Medical personnel would need to give the patient special fluids through an IV.

Insect stings and bites- Most insect stings and bites are not fatal unless the child is allergic. Bee stings leave a stinger when they sting and this should be removed right away. If you can see the stinger, use a credit card to scrape it out. Rinse the area gently with water and soap. Apply an ice pack wrapped in a clean towel or washcloth.

If the child is allergic or stung by a poisonous spider, snake, scorpion, call the emergency services right away.

Knocked-out tooth- If a permanent tooth is knocked out, you must seek dental care immediately. You need to call the dentist or the emergency services right away. You must preserve the tooth until you can reach the dentist or hospital. Things to do to preserve the tooth:

- Never hold the tooth by its root; hold it only by its crown
- Never rinse it with water; chlorine can damage the tooth
- Rinse it gently with milk or saline solution
- Try to push the tooth back to its socket if the child is old enough to hold it there; if not, store it in milk or between your lower gum and cheek.

Nosebleeds- Most nosebleeds are minor and can be stopped by simple intervention. Have the child sit leaning his head forward slightly. Pinch the bottom of his nose for 10 minutes. Check to see if the bleeding stopped after 10 minutes; do not stop and peek in the middle. Hold it for 10 minutes straight. If the bleeding does not stop, try it again for another 10 minutes. If you can not stop the bleeding or there are other symptoms, call the local emergency services.

Poisoning- Poisonous substances can be found throughout every home. These substances can be cleaning fluids, medicines, fertilizers or any other chemicals that should be kept out of a child's sight and reach. If you suspect a child has ingested a poisonous substance, call your local Poison Control Center for help. If you do not have this number handy, call the nationwide Poison Control Center at 1-800-222-1222. Inducing vomiting used to be advised; however, pediatricians do not advise it any longer. If the child is unresponsive or not breathing, call the local emergency services right away.

Seizures- Most brief seizures are non life-threatening. If the seizure lasts more than a few minutes or other symptoms arise, you must call the emergency services. Do not try to stop child from shaking as it will not stop him doing so and cause further discomfort for him. Place him on the carpet on his side. In case if he vomits, his airway won't be blocked. Notify his pediatrician.

Sprains and strains- Sprains are the partial tear of ligaments or tendons. Ligaments connect two bones together and tendons connect the bones to the muscle. Sprain is a partial tear in a muscle. These conditions are usually caused by not stretching or warming up before playing sports. Wearing protective gear when playing sports is also necessary for prevention of sprains and strains.

If you suspect the child has sprained or strained any of his body parts, have the child stop the activity immediately. Swelling in the area is normal; however, if you see other symptoms that indicate a broken bone or infection, you must seek emergency help. Otherwise, minor sprains and strains can be treated at home by following these steps:

- Rest the injured body part until the pain lessens
- Apply ice pack wrapped in a towel for 15 minutes; repeat it 6 to 8 times a day
- Place an elastic compression bandage over the injury for at least two days
- After the first two days, start applying heating pads for three to four times a day

Sunburn- Sunburns are easily preventable by applying a sunscreen SPF15 or higher before going in the sun and wearing protective gear. Sunscreen must be reapplied every two hours if the child is swimming or sweating. Wearing a brimmed hat, sunglasses, and a light t-shirt under the sun protects the child even better; sunscreen should still be applied. As a matter of fact, sun protection is imperative any day of the year. Wearing sunscreen before going outside even on the cloudy days is the best protection from sun damage. If you suspect the child has minor sunburn, minor skin irritation and redness, you should:

- Take the child indoors or on shade away from the sun
- Give the child a cool bath, not cold
- Make sure the child gets enough fluids

If the child has blisters, fever, chills, headaches, dehydration or any other symptoms besides skin irritation and redness, call a doctor.

CPR

Knowing CPR can be a lifesaver and every caregiver should be trained in it. Reading about CPR will give you a general idea about what it is; it does not replace a real CPR training where you practice lifesaving techniques on mannequins. CPR courses are only a few hours and well-worth the time invested. Check with your local American Red Cross or American Heart Association to find a class in your area. These classes can teach you how to recognize an emergency, give rescue breaths, perform chest compressions, and save a choking child. Techniques differ by infants, children and adults. Make sure you are properly trained in the age group of the children you are taken care of. It is also a good idea to repeat the training every few years to keep your knowledge and skills up-to-date.

There are many accidents that may cause child to stop breathing or circulating blood. If you suspect a child is not breathing, you need to call the emergency services right away. You can listen to the breath or watch the child's chest movements to determine whether he is breathing or not. On the spot CPR can help restore breathing and blood circulation to the vital organs until the emergency medical crew arrives. Otherwise, brain damage or death may occur within a matter of minutes.

Three basics (ABCs) of CPR:

- **A is for Airway-** The victim's airway must be open in order for him to breath. Anything that is blocking the airway must be removed. CPR course teaches how to check the airway and clear any obstructions as well as how to position the child for the rescue breaths.

- **B is for Breathing-** If the child is not breathing, rescue breaths should be given through his mouth at the correct intervals. This forces air in to the victim's lungs.

- **C is for Circulation-** Chest compressions may restore blood circulation to the vital organs. CPR courses show how to perform chest compressions on infants and children as well as how to combine them with rescue breaths.

Fire

Importance of fire prevention can not be emphasized enough. Fire is a scary experience that can cause panic, serious injury, or even death. Leading cause of house fires are common household items such as heating devices, bedding, apparel, upholstered furniture, lighters, and matches. Even though these items are being made safer, caution should be used.

Having working smoke alarms throughout the house is the first step to fire safety. Smoke alarms should be checked periodically and the batteries should be replaced as needed. Using electrical appliances as instructed and with care is also important to prevent fire at the first place. Young children should not be allowed near electrical appliances or electrical outlets. Covers for electrical outlets are very popular child-proofing items and can prevent small children stick objects in them. They can prevent fires and electrical shock. Lighters, matches and candles should not be used around children.

Knowing what to do in case of a fire can save lives. This requires some preparation before actually a disaster strikes. Children should actively participate in learning the dangers of fires and practicing fire safety. A fire escape plan should be formulated and children should be trained on what to do in case of a fire with periodic fire drills. A good place to seek help to educate the children about fires is your local fire department. Children like these visits and firemen can answer any questions you and the children may have.

Have an escape plan- Having an escape plan before a fire breaks out is essential. Everyone in the household should learn the easiest and fastest way out of the house in case of a fire as well as where to meet after escaping the fire. Identifying two routes is necessary in case if one is blocked. A meeting place can be a neighbor's house or an open area.

If you are trapped in a room when the fire starts and the door is closed, look for fire signs on the other side of the door before opening it. If you see any of these signs, you should not open the door:

- Is smoke or fire coming through the cracks of the door?
- Is smoke coming from under the door?
- Does the door feel hot or warm?

If there is no smoke coming and the door feels cool, you can open the door slowly and carefully. There is still a chance of fire on the other side. If there is no fire or smoke, go quickly towards the exit through the planned fire escape route. If you feel sudden burst of heat or smoke into the room, close the door immediately. Cover the cracks around the door with sheets or any other clothing to prevent smoke and heat coming in. You can also cover your nose and mouth with a piece of clothing to prevent inhaling smoke. If you have a special fire escape ladder in the room, use it according to the manufacturer's directions to get everyone in the room out of the house. Otherwise, call the local emergency services if you have a phone and open the window to shout for help. Children may tend to hide when they are scared and this may pose a problem if firemen need to rescue them. Teach them to never hide under beds or furniture in case of a fire.

Crawl- Inhaling smoke is the main cause of death rather than flames in majority of fires. It is essential not to inhale smoke while trying to get out of the house. If you see any smoke while escaping from a fire, you should start crawling rather than walking as smoke rises in the air.

If your clothes catch on fire, stop and drop on the floor. Cover your face with your hands and start rolling around until you put out the flames. Do not try to run as air feeds the fire and it will help the flames grow bigger.

Fire extinguishers- Keep a fire extinguisher on each floor of the house in case of small fires. If the fire is very small and you can put it out, take the children to the nearest neighbor's house first. Then, use the fire extinguisher to put out the fire according to the manufacturer's instructions. It is always a smart idea to learn exactly where the fire extinguishers are on each floor and read the instructions before a disaster strikes.

Do not walk back into the house if the fire has gotten bigger or poses a danger to your well-being. Call the local emergency services.

CHAPTER 10 - CHILDHOOD ILLNESSES & CONDITIONS

Information below is provided to familiarize you with common childhood illnesses and conditions. It is not intended as medical advice. You should not attempt to diagnose or cure a child's illness on your own; consequences can be permanently damaging or even fatal to a child. Medicines should be administered only as prescribed and instructed by a doctor.

How to administer medication

Children get sick quite often and you may find yourself in a situation where you need to administer medication to a child. Insist on parents preparing detailed written instructions about how to administer the medicine. Keep a log of how much and when the medicine was given to the child; ask parents to do the same for you when you are off duty. This is very important for the safety of the child and to prevent accidental overdosing. Some important pointers to keep in mind about medications:

- Only give medication as instructed by a doctor or parent
- Do not try to cure an illness on your own; if in doubt, call the doctor or a parent
- Never give a child medicine without his parent's knowledge and approval first

- Store the medicine according to the directions on the package
- Always keep medications out of reach of children
- Take notes about the timing and dosage of the medicines you give
- Always check the expiration date on medications
- Never give anyone medications prescribed for someone else
- Never give children aspirin
- Never call medicine "candy" around a child

ADHD (Attention Deficit Hyperactivity Disorder)

ADHD is a common disorder that affects school-age children. Even though it is more common among boys than girls, there is not a single definite cause of ADHD. Hyperactivity, inability to focus and impulsiveness are symptoms of ADHD. Most children act in a way close to the symptoms of ADHD, but for a child to be diagnosed with ADHD he should show the symptoms before the age of seven more severely than his peers. In addition, the symptoms must be present over a long period of time and in at least two different settings. They would also need to be impairing child's functioning and cause difficulty in school, daycare, home, or social life.

There are three types of ADHD: inattentive, hyperactive, and combined. Symptoms of each one are listed below:

Inattentive type
- difficulty listening when spoken to
- forgetful in daily activities
- easily distracted
- inability to pay attention to details; careless mistakes in schoolwork and activities

104

- difficulty sustaining attention in activities and tasks
- avoidance of tasks that require mental effort
- difficulty following instructions through
- problems with organization
- tendency to lose things like notebooks, toys, pencils, and homework assignments

Hyperactive type
- squirming in seat, fidgeting with hands or feet
- difficulty with remaining seated
- running around or climbing excessively
- seems constantly "on the go"
- interrupting others or intruding
- blurting out answers before question is finished
- talking excessively
- difficulty playing quietly
- difficulty waiting for turns

Combined type
It is the most common type of ADHD and the symptoms are the combination of previous types.

Even though there is no cure for ADHD, there are medications and behavioral treatments to manage it. Doctors can evaluate the child, diagnose and suggest treatment methods. Medications can keep the symptoms under control, but may have some side effects. Behavioral method requires caregivers help the child concentrate by providing him a distraction-free environment, helping him get organized, teaching him good study skills, and creating a comfortable routine for him.

Allergies

Allergy is immune system's overreaction to allergens. Allergens are not harmful to everyone and can be found almost anywhere. Immune systems of the people with allergies react to these substances inappropriately, causing symptoms. These symptoms range from hives, rash, nasal congestion, coughing, wheezing, itchy throat/nose to nausea, diarrhea, and difficulty breathing in case of insect bites. If the child is extremely allergic to a substance, he can develop a severe reaction after he comes in contact with that allergen. Emergency medical care is needed in this case. Symptoms are easily identifiable and may include:

- difficulty breathing
- swelling of face, lips, throat, or tongue
- diarrhea
- hives
- vomiting
- nausea
- unconsciousness
- sudden drop of blood pressure
- tightness in throat

Some allergies are seasonal and affect people during the "allergy seasons" when pollen count is high. Seasonal allergies are caused by exposure to outdoor allergens, such as pollen, grass or weed. Indoor airborne allergens include dust mites, pets, mold, and second hand smoke. Some people show allergic reactions to food, most common ones being peanuts, tree nuts, eggs, cow's milk, soy, fish, shellfish, and wheat. Insect bites, chemicals and medicines can trigger allergies for some as well.

There is no cure for allergies; the best thing to do is to avoid the substances that cause the allergic reactions. The best thing to do if a child is allergic to a certain food is to avoid it. Seasonal allergies can be relieved temporarily by over-the-counter or prescription drugs. When it comes to airborne allergens, the best thing is to provide an environment free of allergens that the child is allergic to. You can do the following to keep an allergen-free environment:

- Vacuum the children's area often
- Keep the windows of the car and the house closed during the allergy season
- Do not use ceiling fans
- Limit outdoor activities during allergy season
- Cover the pillows and the mattresses with special covers
- Keep the pets away from the child
- Keep the humidity indoors low

Appendicitis

The appendix is a three to six inch long structure that is attached to the large intestine. There is no known purpose of appendix and people can live healthy lives without it. However, it must be removed if it becomes inflamed or infected. Otherwise, it can burst and become life-threatening. Symptoms of appendicitis are common symptoms of many other conditions which make it hard to diagnose:

- abdominal pain in the lower right side
- vomiting
- nausea
- poor appetite
- swelling in abdomen
- diarrhea
- low grade fever

Autism

Autism is a developmental disorder that affects how child thinks, behaves, interacts, and communicates. The cause of autism is unknown to this day, but it is usually diagnosed by the time a child turns three years old. Autistic children physically don't look any different than children who are not autistic, which makes it harder to diagnose.

After the first birthday, an autistic child may show some signs of falling behind in the way he talks and interacts with others. For example, failing to gesture, play social games like peek-a-boo, and respond to loud sounds can all be the symptoms of autism. Children with autism may have trouble developing social skills and relations as well as speech problems. Autistic children usually prefer playing alone and are not interested in sharing toys with others. They also have difficulty developing emotional attachments to people, including parents or caregivers. Speech problems can be repetitive speech pattern or speech delays. Below are some of the symptoms of autism, but keep in mind that an autistic child may have only a few of them:

- prolonged tantrums
- avoiding physical contact
- difficulty with affection
- wanting to be alone
- fixation on toys or on rituals
- unusual response to loud sounds
- repetitive rocking or spinning objects
- repetitive speech or lack of speech
- difficulty communicating
- lack of response when spoken to
- crying or laughing for no reason
- under or overactive physically
- difficulty accepting changes in daily routine
- lack of fear

There is no cure for autism although there are medications children can take to keep some of the symptoms under control. Other treatments are usually aimed at improving speech, behavior and social skills through therapy. A doctor who is trained and specialized in treating autism can help create a special program for the child to improve the symptoms.

Chickenpox

Chickenpox is a highly contagious common childhood illness, especially among children under the age of twelve. Children can be given a vaccine between 12-18 months of age to protect them from the illness. Otherwise children develop symptoms within 10-21 days of exposure to the chickenpox virus.

Symptoms often start with fever and decreased levels of activity. After a few days, child develops an itchy rash that slowly covers almost his entire body in the shape of red bumps. These bumps turn into blisters with fluid inside. Then blisters break and turn into sores; sores become crusts. Once a child gets chickenpox, he will have lifelong immunity for the illness. Just as any other illness, child should be watched closely for any complications that may develop.

Although the rash is uncomfortable for the child, doctors won't treat chickenpox with antibiotics as it is caused by a virus. Child should not pick on the blisters to prevent infection. Bathing him in lukewarm water may relieve the itch. The pediatrician or pharmacists can recommend some pain-relieving creams for the itching so that the child won't pick on the blisters. If complications arise or it is a severe case of chickenpox, doctor can prescribe medication.

Colic

Colic is a condition common among newborns. It is characterized by bouts of inconsolable crying for no reason that can last two to three hours at a time. It is a well-known fact that most newborns are fussy. However, a colicky baby cries for hours even if he is healthy and well-fed. It starts around the third to sixth week of life and eventually stops by the time the newborn is three months old.

Definite cause of colic is unknown although there are several theories out there. It could also be particularly difficult to figure out whether the newborn has a medical problem or colic. Caregivers should keep an eye for the symptoms of other illnesses which can also be the cause of crying. Is the baby eating well? Does he have diarrhea or vomiting? Diarrhea and vomiting could signal some other problems. Is he growing well? Colicky babies eat and grow normally. Is he cuddly or irritable when held? If a baby does not like to be held when you are trying to comfort him, there might be something else bothering him.

Dealing with colic can be frustrating as there is no cure or treatment. Try to soothe the baby by cuddling, swaddling, or rocking him. Singing or music may work for some babies as well as walks or warm baths. Taking care of a colicky infant can be an overwhelming experience. Do not shake or rock the baby in frustration under any circumstances as infants' brains can be easily damaged. If you feel frustrated, put the baby down in his crib for a while to catch your breath.

Common cold

Common cold is an upper respiratory infection that usually lasts one to two weeks. Symptoms are runny nose (with yellow or green discharge), sore throat, cough, fever, and sneezing. Due to its contagiousness, a child can get up to eight colds a year; especially if he is a school-age child.

Antibiotics are not used to cure common cold as it is a viral infection. Some over-the-counter drugs such as pain relievers, cough medicines, or nose drops may be recommended by the pediatrician to relieve the symptoms. Plenty of rest, fluids, and avoiding vigorous physical activity can help child recover faster. There are some things that can be taught to children to prevent or decrease the number of colds:

- washing hands thoroughly and often, especially after blowing nose
- staying away from someone with a cold
- not sharing silverware, cups or towels with someone who has a cold
- covering mouth and nose when sneezing and coughing

Croup
Croup is a common infection that usually affects children between the ages of six months and four years old. It is most common in winter and early spring. Croup is associated with a cough that sounds like the bark of a seal and difficulty breathing. Child may have cold-like symptoms in the preceding days; then the cough usually starts in the middle of the night.
To relieve a child with croup, moisture or humidity is the best option. Running a humidifier or running the hot water in the bathroom to create moisture often helps the sick child's breathing.

Diabetes
Diabetes is caused by lack of insulin, a hormone that body needs to use glucose. Glucose is a sugar that is a major source of energy and comes from the foods we eat. Low levels of insulin causes a built-up of glucose. Body of the people with diabetes either can not make insulin,

type I diabetes, or it doesn't work the way it should, type II diabetes. Depending on the type of diabetes and the needs of the child, he will be on a special diet and probably on insulin. Doctors will create a plan to keep his insulin at desired levels. This plan will affect the child's diet and exercise. Symptoms of diabetes include:

- frequent urination
- consuming more fluids than usual
- consuming more food than usual
- losing weight despite eating more than usual

When taking care of a child with diabetes, it is necessary to follow the exact instructions of his doctor and nutritionist to keep the illness under control at all times. You may have to give insulin shots to the child throughout the day, monitor his blood level sugar, limit his sugar intake, prepare balanced meals and monitor his level of physical activity.

Diaper rash

Diaper rash is a very common infection among young infants that cause the skin turn red and sore. Leading cause of diaper rash is not changing the diaper frequently or leaving a soiled diaper on the baby long. However, some babies have very sensitive skin and can react to certain type of baby wipes and diapers as well. They may develop diaper rash even if their diapers are changed frequently.

Rash usually clears within two to three days with frequent diaper changes and baby ointment. If it doesn't go away, spreads, or small red dots appear, pediatrician may have to prescribe a different cream to stop the infection. Caregivers can do a few things when diapering a baby to prevent diaper rash:

- Change the diaper as soon as it becomes wet or soiled
- Dry the baby completely before putting a new diaper on
- Use warm water and soap to clean the baby if he is sensitive to wipes
- Take the diaper off the baby and let him air out as much as you can
- Change any brands of diapers or wipes that might be causing the rash

Diarrhea

Diarrhea is the frequent and watery bowel movements usually accompanied by vomiting. A child with diarrhea needs to get enough fluids in his body to replace the fluids lost. Otherwise, dehydration is inevitable. If the child's stool has mucus or blood or he has fever or prolonged case of diarrhea, child should be evaluated by a doctor.

You can take the following steps to prevent diarrhea:

- wash hands frequently, especially after using the bathroom
- cook eggs, meats, seafood and poultry properly
- do not let juices of raw poultry and meat run into any other food
- clean surfaces and utensils that contact raw meat and poultry
- refrigerate leftovers within two hours of cooking
- rinse fresh fruits and vegetables thoroughly
- do not buy food from the street vendors
- drink bottled water when traveling overseas
- do not drink water from streams, lakes or any other unknown source
- clean toys with water and soap, especially the ones infants put in their mouth

Dyslexia

Dyslexia is a learning disability that makes learning to read difficult even though the child has average or above average intelligence. Children with dyslexia have hard time decoding written language into spoken language. The main cause of this problem is the difficulty recognizing phonemes. Child can not make the connection between the written letters and the sounds they make. Words may look blended together with no spaces or mixed up.

Children with dyslexia do not lack intelligence to achieve in school and pursue a career. They need guidance of specialists to thrive in school and support of adults around them to understand that they are not lazy or stupid and they are working hard to overcome this roadblock.

Ear infection

Middle ear infection, a common illness among young children, is the inflammation of the middle ear area. Children who are around a lot of other children such as in a day care setting are more likely to get ear infections. Tugging or pulling on the ear by infants, pain, fever, and irritability are some of the symptoms of an ear infection.

The pediatrician can determine if the child has an ear infection by examining him. He may prescribe antibiotics or ear drops to treat the infection.

Influenza

Influenza, also known as flu, is a highly contagious respiratory tract infection that is more common in winter. Flu is more common among children than adults although anyone can get it. Due to the fact that flu viruses have different strains, it is hard to prevent. Flu is often mistaken with common cold; however, flu symptoms develop quicker and are more severe than common cold. Symptoms include:

- fever
- chills
- cough
- runny nose
- sore throat
- muscle aches
- loss of appetite
- fatigue
- nausea
- weakness
- vomiting
- diarrhea
- headache

Although antibiotics do not work with flu, drinking plenty of fluids and getting rest help child recover faster. Child must be closely monitored throughout and after the illness as it can lead to pneumonia, bronchiolitis, and croup. These are much more serious illnesses than common cold or flu. Seek medical advice if symptoms worsen or child has other medical conditions.

Measles

Thanks to the MMR vaccine, measles is extremely rare in the developed countries. Measles is a highly contagious respiratory infection that causes red skin rash which covers the whole body. Another marker of the measles is the small red dots with white centers inside the mouth. Other symptoms are very much like flu symptoms.

Roseola

Roseola is a contagious viral illness that is most common among the children between the ages of six months to two years. Initial symptoms are high fever, runny nose and irritability. After three to five days, fever suddenly stops and raised pink rash starts to appear. There is no treatment for roseola; because it is caused by a virus, antibiotics do not work. Controlling the fever can help child feel better.

Scarlet fever

Scarlet fever is caused bacteria which also causes strep throat and will need to be treated with antibiotics. It is contagious and seen most among children under the age of ten. Symptoms are sore throat and fever as well as some of the symptoms of a strep throat. The distinctive sign of scarlet fever is the red rash with tiny red bumps. Skin that is covered with rash may start to peel once the rash fades.

SIDS (Sudden Infant Death Syndrome)

SIDS is the sudden, unexplained death of an infant under one year of age. It is also called as "crib death" as it usually strikes the babies in their crib while sleeping. Experts recommend that babies under one year of age should sleep on their back to prevent SIDS. It is also recommended that babies sleep on a firm mattress with no pillows or toys in the crib. Although there is no definite known cause of SIDS, risk factors include:

- sleeping on stomach or side
- excessive sleepwear on the baby
- smoke exposure during pregnancy and after birth
- babies of mothers younger than twenty years of age
- poor prenatal care

- low birth weight or premature babies

Strep throat

Strep throat is caused by a bacteria and very common among children aged three and above. It is contagious and can easily spread in school or daycare settings by sneezing, coughing and handshaking. Unlike sore throat, which is viral and is not treated with antibiotics, strep throat needs to be treated by antibiotics. Doctor would need to examine the child and do a throat swab to determine if the child has strep throat. Symptoms of strep throat include:

- fever
- red and white patches in the throat
- swollen lymph nodes
- pain in lower abdominals
- loss of appetite
- irritability
- headache

To prevent spread of strep throat, child's towels, eating utensils, napkins should be kept and washed separately. He should also cover his mouth and nose when coughing or sneezing. Importance of hand washing can not be emphasized enough. Without proper hand washing, infection can spread to other people around the sick child easily.

Teething

Cutting of first teeth can be a painful experience for an infant. Often, it is easy to see the signs of teething and discomfort. Drooling, tender gums and chewing on objects are all indicators of teething. The first teeth, two bottom front teeth, start pushing through the gum between the ages of four to seven months. Within the next four to eight weeks, four upper front teeth appear. Usually a child has twenty teeth by the time he is three years old.

Babies' gums should be cleaned with a clean washcloth even before the first tooth erupts. New teeth should be cleaned the same way or with a special infant toothbrush. Toothpaste should not be used in young children as they can not spit it out. If he is too young to spit the toothpaste out, use water only when brushing his teeth. Never let children swallow toothpaste.

Thrush
Thrush is a common infection among infants younger than six months. It is caused by candida yeast. Inside of the mouth, inside of the cheeks and the roof of the mouth look like coated with a white coating. It usually does not cause discomfort; however, doctor can prescribe medication to clear it. Keeping the bottles' nipples and pacifiers clean help prevent reinfection.

CHAPTER 11 - FOOD & NUTRITION

Teaching healthy eating habits to children early in life is an important part of how they will make food choices in the future. Children copy behavior and this includes the eating habits of the major adult figures in their lives. For example, while lecturing the children about the negative effects of soda, consuming it in front of them confuses the children further. Same applies to fruits and vegetables. Unfortunately most children are known to resist fruits and vegetables, number one food group that prevents numerous diseases. The first step to encourage them is to keep different fruits and vegetables around to show them they are a big part of your diet.

Involving children in food shopping and preparation is also a good way to teach them about nutrition and healthy eating. Children like to help in the kitchen. Assign them simple and safe tasks. There will be some mess, but the results will be well-worth it. They will feel a sense of accomplishment and eat the food they help prepare. It is also a great way to improve a child's self-esteem. Furthermore, measuring ingredients and halving or doubling recipes will help them with their math skills.

When introducing solid foods to infants, it is recommended to introduce one new food at a time. This will help you determine if the child is allergic to certain foods. If an infant does not like a new food, you can keep reintroducing the food after a few days. Even if the first attempts don't work, he may suddenly like it after a number of tries.

Establishing healthy eating habits should start at this age. Children will build up their dietary preferences as they grow. A solid foundation must be established at every step of the way.

Things you can do to help children to be healthy eaters:

- Do not force children to eat
- Involve children in food shopping and reading food labels
- Visit orchards and farmer's markets
- Involve children in cooking; give them small, age-appropriate tasks
- Eat healthy, nutritious food to set a good example
- Prepare and offer variety of foods
- Avoid sodas and fruit-flavored drinks loaded with sugar and artificial sweeteners
- Incorporate fruits and vegetables into daily routine
- Offer water and milk instead of soda
- Limit junk food and sweets which have very low nutritional value
- Do not use food as reward or bribe
- Make sure children get their daily exercise balanced with their food intake
- Offer fruits (fresh or dried) and vegetable sticks as snack instead of junk food
- Praise the children when they eat healthy foods
- Be consistent; don't give into a child's nagging by giving him junk food

Tips to get children to eat fruits and vegetables:

- Cut vegetables into interesting shapes

- Offer plain yogurt and cheese as vegetable dipping or dressing
- Talk to children about the importance of fruits and vegetables
- Mix fresh or dried fruits and nuts into cakes, muffins, and breads
- Keep non-perishable fruits on the counter for children to grab easily
- Take them grocery shopping and ask them to pick out fruits and vegetables
- Hide vegetables they dislike in pasta sauces, meat balls, pancakes and soups

Nutrition

Every age group has different nutritional needs. Besides the age of a child, some other factors contribute to the nutritional needs. Children's daily calorie needs increase as they grow. Activity level of a child also contributes to his calorie needs. Children who are very active will need more calories than children who are not. Calorie needs of two children of same age may also differ by their body built. Every child has a different body type; some are larger than the average and some smaller. Let's look into the important nutritional facts of each age group.

Newborn

Up until six months of age, breast milk or iron-fortified formula provides all the nutrients a newborn needs. They don't even require water or juice during this period. Experts agree on the benefits of breast milk and more new mothers try to breastfeed their infants lately. In some cases it may not be possible for a mother to breastfeed her infant for a long period, especially if she needs to go back to work. Some mothers use breast pumps to extract and store the milk for use by caregivers in the bottle. Child still gets all the benefits of the breast milk. In some cases, breast milk may not be available and special iron-fortified infant formula must be used to feed the baby.

During the first and second months, babies usually need on-demand feeding. Make sure to attend their needs timely when they need food. After the first few months, they usually get into a routine and the amount of food they take increases as they get bigger. As a caregiver, you would need to know how to bottlefeed a newborn baby safely. Some points to pay attention when feeding a newborn:

- Children under twelve months of age should never be given cow's milk
- Do not heat the bottles in the microwave
- The best way to heat a bottle is to place it in a container filled with warm water until it is warm enough
- Test the temperature of formula or breast milk on your wrist before feeding
- Avoid playing with a baby vigorously right after feeding
- Never feed a baby leftover formula or breast milk
- Always burp the baby right after feeding
- Small amount of spit ups are normal after feeding
- If the baby vomits large amounts frequently, let the parents know
- Do not prop the bottle when feeding
- Throw away the leftover formula in the bottle to prevent accidental use
- Do not put the baby down on the crib with a bottle
- Clean babies gums with a clean washcloth after feeding
- Sanitize the bottles after use
- Prepare bottles only for use in the next 24 hours or less, each bottle should have formula or breast milk enough for one feeding

- Throw away any refrigerated formula after 24 hours
- Never give anything solid to an infant under four to six months old (best time to start solids depends on infant's readiness for solid food)

Infant

Most infants are ready for solid foods by the time they reach four to six months. Depending on the infant, they may start earlier or later. The first solid food to give a baby is the iron-fortified infant rice cereal mixed with breast milk, formula or water. Do not put the cereal in the bottle; you should feed the baby with a baby spoon. Always introduce a small amount first with any solid food. If the baby likes the food, you can gradually increase the amount given.

Breast milk and/or formula should still be given to infants. Cow's milk, honey, citrus fruits, citrus juices and eggs must be avoided until infant is one year old. Baby can be switched to cow's milk after the first year and/or he can still drink breast milk.

The most important part of introducing solids is to introduce one new food at a time. This will help you watch out for any food allergies infant may have. If you notice any rash on the baby's skin, diarrhea, or fussiness, you should stop feeding that particular food and talk to the parents. Some food allergies may be severe and you should always look out for food allergies when introducing a new food.

Babies' first solid foods must be soft as they don't have enough teeth to grind the food. Pureed vegetables and fruits are great starters. Babies especially like sweet pureed vegetables and fruits such as applesauce, carrots, and sweet potatoes. Whether you make the baby food yourself or use commercial jarred baby food, you should administer good hygiene principles. Wash all vegetables and fruits before making baby

123

food. In order to prevent bacteria build up, do not dip the spoon you are feeding the baby back into the jar. Instead, put some of the food into a little bowl and feed the baby.

Finger food should not be introduced before eight or nine months depending on the infant's readiness. This is the time infants can be introduced to more textured foods. Keep in mind that babies may easily choke on food and watch them closely during feeding. They can start eating chicken and meat as long as they are grinded up into very small pieces. Keep giving mashed vegetables and fruits along with other soft table foods. Soft cheeses and cheerios are good options. Even if everything is cut into small pieces or mashed to prevent choking, children should never be left unattended while feeding.

At twelve months, infants graduate to cow's milk; however, pay close attention to allergies in order to make a smooth transition. Babies should drink whole milk until they are two years old as they need the fat whole milk provides for their development. By now, he should be able to use a sippy cup to drink liquids and it may be a good time to stop using the bottle. He can accompany family dinners sitting on his high chair and eat most of the soft, safe table foods.

Toddler
Toddler years are associated with independence and separate identity. Toddlers establish their presence at the table by eating three meals a day along with adults and feeding themselves. They can start using spoons and forks specially made for toddlers.

Toddlers can usually eat what the adults are eating as long as the food is cut, diced, mashed or grinded. Child's solid food intake will increase and his need for milk will decrease at this stage. If cow's milk is used, whole milk should be given to children under the age of two as low fat milk will not provide all the nutrients he needs for his development. After the second birthday, pediatrician is most likely to approve the switch to 2%, 1%, or skim milk.

Most parents and caregivers worry that toddlers do not eat enough. Although children are typically picky eaters at this stage, forcing a child to eat should be avoided at any age. Toddler's growth rate slows down and is not nearly as fast as an infant's or newborn's growth rate. You should not compare how much he ate then and how much he eats now. It is normal for a toddler to consume less food. He will be fine as long as there are no symptoms of malnourishment. Offer him a variety of foods including all major food groups that toddlers need. When child is being introduced to new foods, he may not accept most them at the first try. The key to success is to keep offering the food again after a while. If you cut up some green beans and the child does not like it at the first try, don't give up hope. However, do not force the child to try it again right away. Wait a week and offer it again. It may take over ten tries to get the child to eat green beans, but all your hard work will pay up if he accepts the food eventually.

Portions should be kept small when serving food to a toddler. If you pile up a plate, he may end up not touching anything on it. Offer each food separately, one at a time in small quantities. You can always serve more food if he is willing to eat more. He can also develop his sense of fullness and stop eating when he is full. This will be very helpful to him in the future to prevent overeating. As always, junk food should be avoided or offered at minimum. Hard food is still a choking hazard at this stage. Watch the child at all times when he is eating and do not offer any hard foods especially hot dogs, hard candy, popcorn, whole grapes, raw carrots, and peanuts.

Preschool

Preschoolers are more cooperative than toddlers. They tend to throw less temper tantrums and like to help around the house. They are also more willing to listen and follow directions which can be very useful to establish good eating habits. They can be involved with small tasks in the kitchen; such as, tearing up the lettuce and preparing snacks. Children should be involved with food preparation tasks appropriate for their age. This will help them eat better, have some control over food and improve their self-esteem. Children are more likely to eat what they prepare. Needless to say, offer nutritious food following the Food Guide Pyramid guidelines recommended for the age group. Preschoolers can be given low fat milk as limiting the fat intake at this stage is recommended. Serving lean cuts of meats and avoiding lots of oil as well as sweets are essential.

Children discover junk food at this stage and will probably beg you for them. Do not give into nagging and limit all junk food; such as, cookies, potato chips, and soda to minimum. Pure fruit juice offers essential vitamins, but should be offered at limited amounts as it fills up the stomach fast. Avoid drinks with little fruit juice and tons of sugar. Sugar helps weight gain which can lead to numerous serious diseases.

A well-balanced diet is very important; however, child should not be forced to eat. Even though it is best to get all the nutrients from food, some pediatricians may recommend vitamin supplements if a child is not getting some of the nutrients from his diet. It is essential to set a good example to children at this stage by eating healthy well-balanced meals yourself. Making meal times a stressful event and nagging about food send the wrong message. Keep offering the child variety of foods and make the meal times pleasant to get the best results. If the child does not eat well during his meal times, prepare healthy snacks to make up for the missed nutrients. Fresh/dried fruits, vegetable sticks, cheese,

126

whole-grain crackers, yogurt, and nuts are all wonderful snacks for children.

School age

Although the calorie intake is lower than adults, school-age children can eat pretty much everything adults eat. They also enjoy helping in the kitchen and learning the basics of cooking. Healthy eating habits and nutritional information of foods can be taught as children are at the age where they are able to get more involved in cooking.

Safety should be the main concern in the kitchen; hot pots, hot pans, stoves, and sharp knives pose danger to all children. School-age children are still immature and should be supervised closely when helping in the kitchen. The best task for this age group is measuring ingredients. This can also help them improve their math skills while learning about cooking and nutrition.

Talk to the children about why fruits, vegetables, whole-grains, and dairy products are so good for health. Tell them about the vitamins in fruits and vegetables; use various colors of vegetables to make it more interesting. Their brains soak up all the information given to them and this knowledge can be very beneficial when they make their own food choices in the future.

Prepare the lunch box together and ask them what they want. Notice if their preferences are affected by the information you have given them. Help them make good choices that can prevent obesity, malnutrition and a number of diseases.

Adolescence

Calorie needs of adolescent children depend on body built, gender and activity level. Boys usually need to consume more calories than girls and so do bigger and active children compared to smaller and less active children. As always, well-balanced nutritional meals and snacks are essential for the growth of the child. Hopefully, the child has learned to make good nutritional choices by now. However, you should educate children about healthy eating continuously.

At this age, children can enjoy cooking even more as they can actively participate in it. Learning how to cook will also be a great asset as they approach college age. Most college students gain weight and knowing how to prepare nutritious foods can prevent them from consuming fast food which has very little nutritional value and high fat.

Food Groups

A well-balanced diet should include all of the major food groups. Amount of servings and calorie needs depend on the age, gender and activity level of the child. Some children, especially adolescents, may have different body built compared to their peers. Children with bigger body types may need more calories in order to ensure proper growth.

Carbohydrates

Carbs, short for carbohydrates, provide the fuel our bodies need. Energy needed for physical activity and organ function comes from carbs. Grains are good sources of carbs and come in two forms, refined and whole grains.

Whole grains in particular are excellent sources of carbs and they should be an important part of everyone's diet. Choosing whole grain products at the supermarket can be a little tricky as most food manufacturers want to pass food low in whole grains as whole grain products. Reading the food labels is a good idea to make sure you are actually buying what you think you are buying. When you read the label, make sure the first ingredient reads "whole grain" or "whole wheat". First ingredient listed on the label is the one that particular food product contains the most. Some examples of whole grain products are: brown rice, bulgur, oatmeal, popcorn, wild rice, and bread products made of whole grains.

Refined grains are milled to improve the texture and shelf life of the product. Fiber, iron and B vitamins are removed from the refined grains during this process. Although most of the refined grain products are "enriched" by placing iron and B vitamins back after processing, dietary fiber is not replaced. White flour, white bread and white rice are the most popular examples of refined grain products.

Current Food Pyramid advises that we get at least half of our grain needs as whole grains.

Protein
Rich sources of protein include meat, poultry, fish, dry beans, eggs, nuts and seeds. Lack of protein can cause growth setbacks, loss of muscle mass, weak immunity, and weak heart as proteins are the building blocks of the body.

One concern about protein is the cholesterol and saturated fats that some of the protein-rich foods contain. Meat is a great example of this. It is an excellent source of protein; however, some cuts of meat contain lots of fat. Try using lean cuts of meat and trim the fat off the meat. Hotdogs, ground beef with high fat content, bologna, salami and bacon are particularly high in saturated fat and should be consumed at moderation if at all.

Vegetables and fruits

The benefits of a diet rich of fruits and vegetables can not be emphasized enough. They are literally the super foods that can prevent several serious chronic diseases. They are low in fat and calories; therefore most people do not have to watch or limit how much fruits and vegetables they consume. In fact, most people do not meet their recommended daily needs. Experts are constantly trying to encourage the public to eat more vegetables and fruits. Variety is also an important point as each one is packed with different types of wonderful nutrients. Choose vegetables from different color groups, dark green, orange, purple, and others.

Trying to get children to eat vegetables and fruits can be a hassle. Don't turn it into a frustrating experience. The best way to encourage children to eat vegetables and fruits is to be a good role model for them. Eat the food you praise about in front of them and they will be curious to taste. Incorporate the vegetables they like into the meals. Offer a variety of vegetables and you will find at least a few they will eat. Involve children in grocery shopping and spend most of your time in the produce section. This is the best place to familiarize the child with vegetables of all colors and shapes. Teaching a child to eat vegetables and fruits would be the best thing you will do for his health.

Dairy

Most common dairy products are milk, yogurt, and cheese. Calcium and vitamin D found in milk and milk products are essential for building and maintaining healthy bones.

Whole milk and most varieties of cheese are high in saturated fat that can raise cholesterol levels. Children under two years of age do need the fats and drink whole milk. However, most children can switch to low fat milk after the age of two.

Fats

Fats should be used sparingly in our daily diets. You can start limiting fats at the age of two, but not before that. Children under two years of age need fats for their development and they should not be limited. Otherwise, there can be serious developmental problems, most important being the neurological development. If the child drinks cow's milk, don't switch to low fat milk before the age of two. Most doctors approve switching to 2% milk after the second birthday.

Most of us think of butter and oil when it comes to fat. However, meat also is a source of fat. When serving meat, trim all visible fat. Olive oil contains good fat; use it whenever you can on salads and cooking instead of butter, margarine and other types of oils. Canola oil is also preferred compared to other oils containing saturated fat and cholesterol.

<u>Food Allergies</u>

Food allergy is the body's reaction to certain food as if the food eaten or contacted is harmful. Body tries to fight the allergen by releasing chemicals. Allergic symptoms are caused by these chemicals. Most common symptoms include itchy skin rash, hives, runny nose, wheezing, abdominal pain, vomiting, swelling and tingling feeling in the throat, mouth or lips.

Most common food allergens:
- peanuts
- milk
- tree nuts
- eggs
- wheat
- soy
- fish

- shellfish

Food allergies may surface when you are introducing a particular food to a child for the first time. That is why trying out one new food at a time is crucial to monitor allergic reactions. If the child shows an allergic reaction, the food can be isolated and avoided.

Cooking for a child with food allergies can be tricky. This means reading the food labels and questioning the ingredients of almost any type of food. If a child is allergic to peanuts, you must watch out for any traces of peanut or peanut oil on the food labels or ingredients. Most prepackaged foods can be cross-contaminated during preparation in big facilities. Chocolates prepared in a facility where peanuts are processed can pose as big of a risk as peanuts due to possible cross contamination. Egg allergies prevent a child eat cakes, cookies, and other baked goods unless they are made at home without any eggs. You should also pay extra attention to cross contamination when you prepare food at home. Food allergies can not be treated and the best thing is to avoid the allergen food completely, including skin contact with the food.

Some of the things you can do to avoid food allergies:

- Keep the allergens out of child's meals and sight
- Practice good kitchen hygiene; do not cross contaminate
- Read the food labels and learn the ingredients to avoid
- Teach the child about allergies if his age permits
- If eating out, let the cook know about the allergy
- Keep doctor recommended allergy medication handy
- If allergy is severe and epinephrine is prescribed, keep several of them within easy reach in case of a severe allergic reaction

CHAPTER 12 - DISCIPLINE & BEHAVIOR

Discipline

Discipline is not physical punishment; it is a way to teach children self-control. Discipline should be age-appropriate and persistent. It is important that all caregivers agree and apply the parent-approved discipline methods consistently. If nanny follows the parents' guidelines and mother who comes home tired from work gives into the whining child, child would get mixed messages. He will be mad at the nanny who is working hard to discipline him and all the hard work will have to start all over again.

It is imperative that you discuss the discipline techniques family uses at the interview. If you strongly disagree with the parents' way of discipline, it is better you move on to the next interview. Naturally, spanking or hitting the children are not disciplining and should never be used by anyone. Physical punishment does not contribute towards improving a child's behavior. On the contrary, such violent behavior teaches children that it is okay to hit someone. Instead, positive approaches work the best when it comes to teaching a child good behavior. Try not to concentrate on a child's negative behavior and praise good behavior. Some people are so wound up with negatives they often forget to see the positive behavior. Don't be afraid to say "good job!" often.

Infant

Infants don't misbehave intentionally. However, once they start crawling, they try to get into everything in sight. That is why childproofing the infants' environment is so important. Providing a safe and secure area will help the child explore and learn. If they get into a dangerous activity, it is better to redirect their attention to a different activity. If an infant wants to get into a kitchen cabinet that he is not allowed to, remove him from the area and offer him one of his toys. Do not reprimand him for trying to explore the world. Instead, focus and praise good behavior. This will also help the child's self-esteem.

Toddler

For a toddler who has abundance of curiosity and will, temper tantrums are almost an inevitable part of life. When appropriate discipline techniques are used, they start to occur less frequently.

Toddlers like to explore their surroundings and test their limits. They want to find out what they can get away with. Temper tantrums are toddlers' way of showing their frustration. Yelling at a toddler certainly will not solve any problems other than teaching him that it is okay to yell. You must keep in mind that temper tantrums are a part of this stage and remain calm. You can ignore and not pay attention to tantrums where the child is simply seeking attention for no reason. Avoid power struggles and try to explain to them what they can and can not do. Toddlers can follow simple instructions. You can even start explaining to them the consequences of their behavior. For example, if he throws his toy out the window, it will break and he can't play with it anymore.

If the behavior becomes too disruptive, time-out can be used. Time-out is to remove the child from the environment to a boring or neutral area in the house for a short period of time. One minute of time-out for every year of life is usually the rule of thumb. Place the child in a chair or the bottom of the stairs and wait until he calms down. Do not talk to him or let him watch TV during time-out. He should be in an isolated area where you can still watch him to make sure he is safe and sound.

Preschool
Preschool age children can understand rules and follow simple directions better than toddlers. First of all, you should start teaching the child what behaviors are appropriate. You should also explain what the rules, for example the house rules, are. Unless someone tells the child about these things, it is not fair to expect him to know them. For example, don't expect the child to know about bicycle safety without explaining to him about the importance of wearing a helmet. You should also explain to him the reasoning behind wearing a helmet and the consequences of not wearing one. Be consistent and patient, you will see the results.

He may still throw tantrums when frustrated and do time-out when things get out of control. To prevent or minimize negative behavior, be sure to spend time with him, talk to him, and answer his questions. If you act calm, he is more likely to behave better.

School-age
Now that the child knows more about the rules and appropriate behavior, you can expect him to follow them better. Children of this age should be taught to deal with the consequences; for example the consequences of not finishing homework on time. He will probably have a first hand experience and will know not to repeat such behavior.

Grounding and withholding privileges are also used with school-age children. Make sure to follow up on what you say. If you tell the child he can not play before finishing homework, make sure the homework is finished before playtime. Do not make unrealistic statements such as "You will never ride your bike again if you don't eat your dinner".

Adolescence

By now, children know what is expected of him. However, he will still test his limits as he gains his independence. He will also need his privacy which you should respect, but he will still need guidance and approval. Role models and adults in his life are very important to him. Guide him in the right direction about important issues rather than nagging him about unimportant things. He should start learning making the right decisions for himself at this stage. That does not mean that rules about important things such as homework should be bent. Do not criticize too much and praise good work just as in any stage of childhood. Withholding privileges such as video games or TV time is an effective discipline technique at this stage as the child is well-versed with consequences by now.

<u>Discipline Techniques</u>

By the time you start a new job, chances are parents have established some sort of discipline techniques that work with their children. You would be expected to follow their rules when it comes to disciplining their children. Remember that it is very important for all parents to be consistent with disciplining. If parents want you to use time-outs when the toddler gets out of control, you should apply it as instructed. Hopefully, parents realize that they have to follow their own rules as well. Some of the common discipline techniques include:

Positive reinforcement
Positive reinforcement is a discipline technique where you concentrate and praise good behavior instead of focusing on bad behavior. Some people can be quick to criticize the children's bad behavior and they don't acknowledge the good behavior often enough. See the good things the child does and praise appropriately to reassure the child. Appropriate praising help children build self-esteem.

Distraction/redirecting
Children will do things they are not supposed to. It is a part of growing up. Redirecting technique is simply directing the child's attention to a positive activity or behavior. For example, if you have a toddler who wants to ride his seven-year-old sister's bicycle, you can redirect his attention to a toy that is appropriate for his age.

Time-out
Time-out is to send the child to a neutral area in the house where he sits alone without any interaction for a brief period of time. Make sure there is no TV or toys in the time-out area. Most people designate a time-out chair in the house and place the child on the chair until he calms down. One minute for every year of age is a good rule of thumb. For example, if he child is three-years-old, he can sit for three minutes.

Consequences
It is essential to give children some control over the decisions they make. By explaining the consequences of their actions, you provide them the tools they need to develop good judgment skills. Only then, child can start learning how to make good decisions and deal with the consequences of bad behavior. This technique works well with school-age children.

Withholding privileges

Withholding privileges technique is to remove something that child values due to negative behavior. This could be anything that child values high; such as, watching TV, playing video games, or playing in the playground after school. This technique is usually effective with school-age children and older. It should not be used frequently for it to be effective.

Temper Tantrums and Self Control

Temper tantrums can be overwhelming even for the most patient nannies. Tantrums are usually caused by stressful situations, for example, a toddler can throw a tantrum if he can't figure out how his new toy works or a kindergartener can do it in the grocery checkout line because you didn't buy her candy. Children need to learn some degree of self-control in order to overcome a stressful situation. They need to realize crying and screaming will not get them what they want.

Set a good example by not yelling or loosing your temper when a child acts up. If he sees you screaming, he will think that it is okay to scream. Do not give into tantrums by bending the rules. If you are embarrassed by a tantrum in a crowded grocery store, take the child to a quiet corner until he is calm instead of giving in and buying the candy he has been screaming about. If you give in, the child will learn that throwing a tantrum is the most effective way for him to get the candy. If you remove him from the environment and put him to time-out, he will learn that this kind of behavior brings an undesirable outcome. He will learn the consequences of his behavior and control his outbursts and tantrums.

Building Self-Esteem

Self-esteem is how a person perceives himself or herself. It is the opinions and feelings we have about ourselves. Building a child's self-esteem starts early on in life and the lack of it can cause major problems in the future. A child with low self-esteem can have trouble dealing with problems and difficult situations throughout his life. He may not see himself as an able person who can overcome obstacles and become dependent on others. He may grow up as a person who is influenced by others easily and can not make good decisions for himself.

Self-esteem starts developing during infancy. First senses of accomplishments; such as, rolling over or being able to crawl reassure the child that he can do things on his own. The best way to help a child build a healthy self-esteem is to encourage the child to explore new things and praise accomplishments. This type of can-do attitude gives the child the boost he needs to succeed. Of course, adults would need to have realistic expectations from the child in order to build healthy self-esteem. Praises should not be so frequent that they lose meaning. They should be descriptive of what the child has done well, including the process not only the result.
Children also need to feel that they are loved. Affection from the significant adults in their lives gives them the assurance that they are loved. Only then, they can have the confidence to build their self-esteem. Criticizing should be kept to minimum; do not criticize little things. Being over criticized can hurt children's self-esteem and discourage them to try new things.

CHAPTER 13 - ACTIVITIES & PLAY

Reading to children

Starting to read to children at an early age is one of the best gifts you can give them. Don't wait until the right age to start reading books out loud. Children of any age like the interaction and the sound of your voice, even a newborn. You may feel like infants don't understand or gain anything from reading out loud because you may not see the results right away. However, reading to a baby can help child learn sounds, colors, and shapes even if they don't understand the whole story. Child starts to learn the building blocks of reading by listening to you read.

The best first books are usually bright, colorful books that can familiarize the child with sounds and objects. Babies like the books they can touch and feel. There are several such books with furs, mirrors, and pop ups. Books with colorful simple pictures in the middle and books with rhyming text are also ideal for infants.

In early years, you will end up reading the same book over and over again. You might wonder if there are any benefits of reading the same book to a child. The answer is yes. It takes a while for young children to get a hang of the book. They don't understand what you read the first time and repeating the same book helps them understand it better. If you are reading a book about shapes, it may take many repetitions for the child to make the connection between the shapes and the sounds they are associated with.

Always make sure children of any age have plenty of books around them. If they are surrounded with books, they will want you to read them more and the best way to raise a future reader is to read to the child first. Take trips to the library. They have story hours for almost every age group. Set aside time for reading every day. Half an hour before naps or bedtime is usually the best time to read.

Point out the lines on the book as you read so that the child can see the written words read to him. Make the books more interactive by asking questions about what you read. The early books usually contain letters and words to teach children the sounds. Ask child to point out the letters and the objects in the book. Babies have a short attention span, but it improves by age. As you progress into the story books, ask the child to summarize the stories you read. Ask questions about the characters in the book. Stories will help child's imagination and boost his creativity. Ask him to reenact the story or paint pictures about the story.

Even after a child learns how to read, he needs encouragement to be a good reader. If a school-age child wants to read books on his own, pick up your book and set a good role model. Ask him to read aloud to you sometimes. Discuss the books he reads and point out the new words learned. Start building his vocabulary by encouraging him to ask about the words he learned from the book. Reading can be lots of fun once children learn how to read. There is a great amount of information for them to discover and books are the best way to do this. Encourage children to read every day. Don't make it sound like a chore. Instead, teach them reading is fun and relaxing.

Play

Play is an essential part of child development. Through play children learn social skills, communication, creativity, and sharing. Just like reading, play should start at infancy. Although it may seem that infants can't give much feedback, they do respond to active play within their capability. Peek-a-boo is a good example of one of the early games. Infant responds back to peek-a-boo by smiling and laughing. He will also respond to other facial expressions or sounds. This shows that his development is well on its way. He responds to the voices and likes to hear the voice of his caregivers. He can focus and follow rattles and other toys as you move them around slowly. Sing soothing lullabies and talk to the baby. You may feel like you are talking to yourself, but babies absorb information given to them. They need to hear the people around them talk in order to start understanding the language.

As infants learn to walk and transform into curious toddlers, their motor skills improve. They become more active and can do more things physically. Improved hand-eye coordination opens the way for more creative activities such as coloring, doing puzzles, and stacking blocks. Increased level of physical activity brings the need for better adult supervision. Toddlers are typically very active and should be encouraged to be so. However, don't let them go without proper rest to avoid tantrums. Make sure they get enough food and rest to go along with their activity levels.

Structured play led by an adult is fun and educational for toddlers, especially when they start to talk. They can communicate and participate better in structured play. Every toddler needs some time of structured play for proper cognitive development. Make the best of this time to teach the toddler valuable skills; such as, sharing, taking turns, and following instructions. He will need these skills when he steps into more social settings.

Unstructured play, also called free play, is also very valuable and necessary for any age-group. During unstructured time, children can use their imagination and creativity. Set up some free play time everyday with adequate supervision. Watch and see how the child is entertaining himself. Monitor his skills with toys and puzzles to see if he is mastering his skills. Praise his efforts and progress. Be specific with your praises; don't give empty ones. Tell them what you liked specifically. Do not only focus on the end product. It is the effort that counts and praising the effort encourages child to try new things.

Toddler years are also the time when play dates can be set to introduce children to other children of his age group. They may not be interested in sharing toys or playing together most of the time. Let them play side-by-side. This is called parallel play and still has its benefits. They can only progress to social play when they have other children around. Guide them on sharing, taking turns, and creative play.

Preschoolers and school-age children enjoy the company of their friends. By now, they know how to share and take turns and can participate in group games. They like the company of their peers more and play better with each other. School-age children progress into group sports such as baseball and basketball. Trips to the playground, library, zoo, and museums are all fun and educational activities. Keep in mind that children of all ages must be supervised during play. This is even more true so for outdoor play; children should not be left alone outside under any circumstances. If you are taking a trip to the library or museum, never let the child out of your sight. It is easy for children to drift away on a field trip, especially in crowded public places.

Toys

Toys are an essential part of children's development. There is countless number of toys in the market today; however, toys should never replace the personal attention a child needs from his caregivers. Toys are the tools for a child to learn and have fun, but they should not be used to babysit the children for several hours. Every child needs some sort of structured play each day lead by an adult. Getting on the floor with children to help them learn and explore is a necessary part of the daily routine. Human interaction is more important than the number of toys a child has. This special time also helps you establish a stronger bond with the child.

Safety is the biggest concern with the toys. All toys must be age-appropriate and safe. Manufacturers test and label the toys; however, you can't only rely on their measures. Many of the toys are recalled each year due to defects; you are the best judge of the toys when it comes to safety. Children must be supervised when playing with toys, especially younger children. Toys should be durable and should not break into small pieces. Every year, several children visit the emergency rooms due to toy-related injuries. Teething infants like to put toys in their mouth. Make sure the toys are bigger than the child's mouth to prevent choking. Don't give babies anything they can swallow. If there are older children's toys around, keep the baby away from them.

Each and every toy should be checked periodically to make sure they are intact. Worn out toys should be thrown away; don't hand them down to other children. Toys should be cleaned often, especially the ones infants tend to put in their mouths. Warm water and soap should get the dirt out of many plastic toys followed by rinsing and drying.

Help children put the toys away at the end of the day to prevent accidental tripping over the toys. Toys left on the floor can even cause adults to trip over and fall, resulting in injury. Nowadays, most children have more toys than they can play with. Rotate them periodically to take advantage of all the toys available. Don't keep all the toys in the play area at all times. Take out as many toys as he can play for a few weeks, then put them away in a closet and take out a new batch.

Children will appreciate their toys better and make the most of each toy.

Music
Children love listening to music and singing along. Even the youngest babies respond to soothing lullabies; it makes them relax and fall asleep. As they grow older and start to understand the lyrics, they can act and sing along the songs. Experts agree that music is an integral part of child's cognitive development. Make music a part of the daily life, expose children to different types of music. Local libraries are a great source for children's music tapes and CDs. Check out some music along with the books when you visit the library. Children can learn to appreciate music at an early age and will be more interested in playing a musical instrument when they are ready.

Homework
Doing homework is the children's first step towards responsibility. It teaches children how to manage time and finish what they start. These essential skills are necessary to prepare children for the work place.

Creating a quiet and comfortable environment for homework is very important. Make sure there are no distractions; turn off the television, computer, and video games before sitting down for homework. Everything the child may need to do his homework should be within his reach.

Naturally, you shouldn't do the homework for him, but you should be available to answer any questions he may have. He may need guidance on finding answers; teach him how to find the information instead of telling him the straight answers. Internet is a great place to do research when used wisely. Be sure the child doesn't access inappropriate sites or get side tracked. Teach him how to use the Internet to his benefit.

Internet usage

Internet can be a great learning tool for any age if used properly. However, not everything available on the Internet is appropriate for children. Therefore, children's internet usage must be closely supervised. There are software programs that can be installed on the computers to block children's access to inappropriate web sites. Even if you trust the child with his internet habits, aggressive internet marketing now brings these web sites in front of anyone. It is best to take some measures to protect the children beforehand.

Internet offers a wealth of good information and children can instantly access this information when doing homework. Teach children good research habits and where to look for solid sources of information.

TV - Video Games

Watching television and playing video games for long periods of time are blamed for weight and behavioral problems in children. This is bad news for children's healthy development. Although right TV programs and video games can be fun and educational, the amount of time children spend in front of them should be minimized. Playing and reading should be on top of the list of activities for children.

CHILD DEVELOPMENT QUIZ

1) When do infants usually start rolling over?
   a) 1 month
   b) 2 months
   c) 3 months
   d) 5 months

2) When do infants usually get their first tooth?
   a) 1-2 months
   b) 3-4 months
   c) 5-7 months
   d) 12 months

3) When do infants usually start sitting without support?
   a) 7-8 months
   b) 3-4 months
   c) 2-3 months
   d) 1-2 month

4) When a toddler throws a temper tantrum:
   a) ignore his behavior
   b) use diversion to divert his attention
   c) avoid confrontation
   d) all of the above

5) When a baby starts crying, it is best to:
   a) ignore him

b) check his diaper
c) offer him a bottle
d) b and c

6) The best way to support and encourage a baby who is just starting to walk:
a) put him in a baby walker
b) put him in a play pen
c) remove the obstacles around and provide a safe environment
d) put him on a high chair

7) What is the best way to encourage children to read?
a) read to them daily
b) buy them a lot of books
c) let them play with the books
d) take them to the library every day

8) Singing to a child:
a) improves his musical skills
b) is useless
c) improves his language skills
d) none of the above

9) Playing with children and doing art projects together:
a) helps their development
b) is useless, children should play alone
c) is a great way to communicate and teach children
d) a and c

10) What do you do when a child refuses to do his homework?
a) let him watch television
b) explain to him he needs to do his homework
c) let him play with his toys
d) give him candy to do his homework

11) What do you do when a child refuses to eat?
a) force him to eat
b) don't force him to eat
c) feed him what he likes even if it's junk food
d) none of the above

12) Discipline is:
a) punishment
b) teaching children self-control
c) must be practiced by parents only
d) not a nanny's responsibility

13) When communicating with children
a) criticize him
b) listen to him
c) show respect for him
d) b and c

14) Which one is true?
a) Children only see their parents as role models
b) Children also see their nannies as role models
c) Children copy only good behavior
d) Children copy only bad behavior

15) When watching television or on the computer
    a) TV hours and programs must be limited
    b) Children should be allowed to watch what they want
    c) Children can use the computer as long as they want without supervision
    d) Children can not be taught good television and computer habits

16) Discipline works when:
    a) Parents and nanny agree and form a united front together
    b) Parents and nanny apply their own methods
    c) Parents and nanny criticize the children
    d) Children are punished

17) When talking to children, it is OK to:
    a) talk in a threatening manner if the child is acting up
    b) to call him bad if he has done something wrong
    c) not to ridicule the child under any circumstances
    d) lose patience and scream

EMERGENCIES & FIRST AID & CPR QUIZ

1) What is the phone number to call in case of an emergency?
   a) 411
   b) 911
   c) area code + 911
   d) local police

2) When an infant is choking, you need to:
   a) call the parents
   b) use the Heimlich Maneuver
   c) take the baby to the hospital
   d) lay the baby face down along your forearm, support her head and shoulders and give 5 sharp slaps between her shoulder blades.

3) In case of a fire, you must first:
   a) try to find the fire extinguisher to put out the fire
   b) gather the children, leave the house and then call 911
   c) call the parents
   d) call 911

4) What is the ABCs of CPR?
   a) Airway - Breathing – Circulation
   b) Airway – Breathing – Cold
   c) Act – Blood – Call 911
   d) Airway – Blood – Cuts

151

5) What must be in a first aid kit?
   a) Sterile gauze and bandages
   b) Diapers
   c) Food
   d) Juice

6) 9-year old child in your care falls and hits his head. He is breathing, but unconscious. What should you do?
   a) call 911 or local emergency number
   b) call his parents
   c) call his doctor
   d) wait and see if he gains consciousness

7) When a school-age child is choking:
   a) drive him to the hospital
   b) do the Heimlich Maneuver
   c) call his parents
   d) do mouth-to-mouth resuscitation

8) When a child's nose is bleeding, first thing to do:
   a) tilt his head back
   b) drive him to the hospital
   c) call 911
   d) have him lean forward and pinch the buttom of his nose until it stops bleeding

9) For minor burns, it is best to:
   a) put toothpaste over the area
   b) put ice over the area

c) run cold water over the area
d) do nothing

10) The child cuts his finger and bleeding a lot, it is best to:
a) call 911
b) put ice on the cut
c) put his hand below his heart
d) put a sterile gauze on the area and apply pressure

FOOD & NUTRITION & FOOD SAFETY QUIZ

1) After you fed the baby formula, she goes down for a nap. When the baby wakes up you realize there is still formula left in the bottle. What would you do with that formula?
   a) Refrigerate it immediately
   b) Feed the baby with it if it smells OK
   c) Discard the formula right away
   d) Keep the formula for the next feeding

2) When can babies start drinking cow's milk?
   a) 6 months old
   b) 9 months old
   c) 10 months old
   d) 12 months old

3) Which foods should be avoided for children under 12 months old?
   a) cow's milk
   b) egg whites
   c) honey
   d) all of the above

4) Which of the below should not be given to children?
   a) raw or runny eggs
   b) cookie dough
   c) rare hamburger
   d) all of the above

5)   Children over the age of 2 can:
        a) Go on a diet to lose weight
        b) Cut all fats from their diet
        c) Limit saturated fats
        d) Eat rare hamburgers

6)   Chicken should be cooked:
        a) Until the thermometer reads 180F and juices run clear
        b) Outside looks cooked
        c) Outside looks dark
        d) Five minutes

7)   Hamburgers should be cooked:
        a) Until the thermometer reads 160F
        b) Inside is pink
        c) Outside looks brown
        d) Five minutes

8)   Fresh fruits and vegetables:
        a) do not need to be washed
        b) must be rinsed thoroughly
        c) can be cut on the same cutting board after cutting meat
            and poultry
        d) always should be cooked before serving children

9)   A healthy diet for school-age children consists of:
        a) milk and meat
        b) processed or canned food
        c) a pure vegetarian diet

d) balanced portions of fresh vegetables, meat, fish, poultry, whole grain products, low fat dairy and fruits

10) After grocery shopping in a hot day, what should be the next thing you do?
   a) Keep the groceries in the trunk of the car until you finish all your errands
   b) Go home and refrigerate the groceries right away
   c) Don't need to refrigerate as long as the packaging is OK
   d) Take children to the playground before going home

11) What is the correct method to thaw frozen food?
   a) Put the food on the kitchen counter the night before
   b) Put the food in hot water
   c) Move the food from the freezer to the fridge
   d) Put the food on the kitchen counter in the morning

12) Leftovers must be:
   a) Kept in the room temperature
   b) Refrigerated within two hours of cooking
   c) Reheated thoroughly before serving
   d) b and c

13) To avoid cross-contamination:
   a) Wash hands before, during and after preparing food
   b) Wash hands, cutting boards, utensils, kitchen surfaces, plates that have contacted raw meat and poultry
   c) Do not let raw poultry juices touch other food
   d) All of the above

PARENT – NANNY RELATIONSHIP QUIZ

1) Key to a successful parent-nanny relationship is
    a) well-behaved children
    b) flexibility of the nanny to accommodate the parents
    c) communication
    d) to ignore the problems

2) Methods of communication can be
    a) weekly meetings
    b) daily logs
    c) performance evaluations
    d) all of the above

3) A mother you work for comes home late after work several times and it is bothering you. How do you resolve this?
    a) Ignore the problem
    b) Rearrange your after work schedule
    c) Talk to her
    d) Talk to your nanny friends about it

4) You are working with a mother who works from home. Your 3-year old charge wants to spend time with her mom instead of staying with you.
    a) ignore the problem
    b) give the child some cookies to stay with you
    c) talk to the mother about the problem
    d) tell the mother she needs to go to the office

5) Written nanny work agreement
a) is not needed
b) does not protect the nanny
c) must be drawn by an attorney
d) is a must have documentation

6) Your employer comes to you about a problem regarding an issue about your childcare methods. What should you do?
a) be defensive
b) listen objectively and understand the problem
c) never accept any blame
d) start criticizing their childcare methods

7) Regarding disciplining the children
a) apply the parent's methods
b) spanking is not discipline and should not be used
c) apply your own discipline methods regardless of what the parents instructed you
d) a and b

8) Parents you work for argue a lot lately, you should
a) keep providing great care for the children
b) try to resolve the parent's problems
c) talk to your nanny friends about this
d) talk to their relatives and see if they can help the parents

9) You drive a car provided by the family. You also use it for your personal trips.

a) provide your own gas for personal trips
b) have the car usage rules spelled out in the work agreement
c) keep the car clean
d) all of the above

10) Parents you work for add more duties without discussing them with you. What should you do to handle this situation?
a) tell them they are violating the work agreement in a non-threatening way
b) tell them additional responsibilities must be discussed first and pay must be adjusted
c) do not say anything and take on the extra responsibilities
d) a and b

SAFETY QUIZ

1)   A safe crib for an infant under 12 months old must have:
       a) a firm, tight fitting mattress
       b) pillows and sheepskins
       c) a soft mattress
       d) comforter or quilt

2)   To prevent SIDS, a baby should sleep:
       a) on his face
       b) on his side
       c) on his back
       d) any of the above

3)   It is safe to put an infant down for a nap on a:
       a) beanbag
       b) waterbed
       c) adult bed
       d) none of the above

4)   When heating a baby bottle, it is best to:
       a) heat it in the microwave
       b) place the bottle in a container filled with warm water
       c) test the liquid on your arm before feeding the baby
       d) b and c

5)   When bathing an infant:

a) test the bath water with your elbow before placing the baby in it
b) gather everything you may need within your reach before bringing the baby in to the bathroom
c) never leave the baby unattended
d) all of the above

6) When you put a baby on a high chair:
a) place the high chair away from the table, counter or wall so that she can't push off from them
b) always buckle the waist and crotch restraints
c) never allow the baby to stand up on a high chair
d) all of the above

7) When can an infant face forward in a car seat?
a) 6 months
b) 12 months and 20 pounds
c) 12 months
d) 20 pounds

8) A booster seat must be used for children until he is:
a) 4 feet 9 inches tall
b) 8 years old
c) either a or b
d) 5 years old

9) A child under the age of 3 should not play with:
a) coins
b) uninflated or broken ballons

c) toys with little pieces
d) all of the above

10) When can a child ride in the front seat of a car?
   a) 12 years old
   b) 10 years old
   c) 8 years old
   d) 6 years old

11) Bicycle helmets should be worn when the child is:
   a) riding on the driveway
   b) riding on the street
   c) any age
   d) all of the above

12) A child in the pool will be OK if:
   a) he knows how to swim
   b) there is a lifeguard present
   c) he is in the shallow end of the pool
   d) none of the above

13) When changing a baby's diaper on a changing table:
   a) never leave the baby unattended
   b) strap the baby to the changing table
   c) gather everything you need before putting the baby on
       the changing table
   d) all of the above

14) To prevent choking:
   a) cut food into bite size pieces
   b) do not feed infants whole hotdogs, peanuts, hard candy or whole grapes
   c) do not let the child play or run while eating
   d) all of the above

15) You have 2 children in the car and need to pick up milk from the store.
   a) They can wait in the car if they are over 7 years old
   b) Unload the children and take them in to the store with you
   c) They wait in the car if it is not too cold or hot outside
   d) If the older child is over 8 years old, ask him to watch the younger child while you run in to the store quickly

16) You are watching an infant and a 6 year old. The older child wants to go out and play while the baby is taking a nap.
   a) Let him go out and stay home with the baby
   b) Leave the baby in the house and watch him
   c) Explain him you can not leave the house when the baby is sleeping and you can not let him go out alone
   d) Ask a neighbor to keep an eye on him

17) You are driving with your infant charge in the car. She drops her toy on the floor and starts crying loudly. What would you do?
   a) Pull the car to the side of the road when it is safe to pick up the toy
   b) Keep driving and ignore her loud cry

163

c) Turn the music up so that you are not distracted with her cry

d) If the traffic is light, turn around quickly to pick up the toy

ANSWERS

Child Development Quiz

1-d	2-c	3-a	4-d	5-d	6-c	7-a
8-c	9-d	10-b	11-b	12-b	13-d	14-b
15-a	16-a	17-c				

Emergencies & First Aid & CPR Quiz

| 1-b | 2-d | 3-b | 4-a | 5-a | 6-a | 7-b |
| 8-d | 9-c | 10-d | | | | |

Food & Nutrition & Food Safety Quiz

| 1-c | 2- d | 3-d | 4-d | 5-c | 6-a | 7-a |
| 8-b | 9-d | 10-b | 11-c | 12-d | 13-d | |

Parent-Nanny Relationship Quiz

| 1-c | 2-d | 3-c | 4-c | 5-d | 6-b | 7-d |
| 8-a | 9-d | 10-d | | | | |

Safety Quiz

1-a	2-c	3-d	4-d	5-d	6-d	7-b
8-c	9-d	10-a	11-d	12-d	13-d	14-d
15-b	16-c	17-a				

14504638R00100

Made in the USA
Lexington, KY
02 April 2012